*F*ollow the *P*iper

Through True Life Stories of a Century

Shared by Seniors from
The Good Samaritan Society – Prairie Creek
Sioux Falls, SD

Edited by Keith Jensen

Shapato Publishing, LLC
Everly, Iowa

Published by: Shapato Publishing
PO Box 476
Everly, IA 51338

ISBN: 978-0-9833526-1-7
Library of Congress Control Number: 2011922707
Copyright © 2011 The Prairie Creek Piper Leadership Committee

All rights reserved. No part of this book may be reproduced or transmitted in any form or by any means, electronic or mechanical, including photocopying, recording, or by an information storage and retrieval system, without permission in writing from the publisher.

First Printing May 2011

One of the remarkable qualities of the story
is that it creates space.

We can dwell in a story, walk around,
find our own place.

The story confronts,
but does not oppress;

The story inspires,
but does not manipulate.

The story invites us to an encounter, a dialog,
a mutual sharing.

From ***The Living Reminder*** by
Henri J. M. Nouwen

ACKNOWLEDGMENTS

The Leadership Committee and their committee members did a lot of heavy lifting to bring this book to fruition. We thank them not only for their work, but also for their creative thinking and support:

    Caroline Schoon, Assistant Editor
    Lynn Bethke, Technical Editor
    Judy Ryan, Art and Graphics Editor
    Dale Harris, Number Cruncher Editor

Jodie Jensen, who owns **The Snapshot** at Lennox, South Dakota, provided all the individual pictures by the biographies. Thank you, Jodie.

Erin Solko, from the Good Sam corporate office, was always available with professional assistance when we rookies needed some good help. Our book is better because of you, Erin. Thank you.

Judy Ryan designed and painted the cover for "Follow the Piper." Thank you for all the help you so freely gave. You are a blessing.

    Keith Jensen, Editor

"When an old person dies, it's like a library burning."
                                                    Alex Haley

FOREWORD

The authors of our book consider themselves the third generation in the upper Midwest prairie. Our grandparents received a lot of deserved attention as the first generation. Many of them came from Europe and built themselves sod huts and plowed the prairie. Our parents improved the land and living conditions. Tom Brokaw named them "The Greatest Generation." We are the third generation and we have a story to tell to our children and grandchildren; and it is important to us that we tell it because we believe our contribution to the prairie is laudable.

While this book is neither psychology nor sociology, it is meant to give the reader historical vignettes of who we are. It is with respect to our parents and the prairie that we tell about our time on the prairie and wherever our lives took us.

Follow the Piper

Through True Life Stories of a Century

TABLE OF CONTENTS

Acknowledgments	5
Foreword	7
Words Pastor Elroy Skaar	17
Roots Into Wings Norm Eitrheim	19
Practicing Medicine Before Cell Phones Dr. Tom Ludgate	23
Grandpa's Christmas Caboose Rocky Ryan	27
The Cat From Southside Chicago Mick Pickford	31
A Norwegian Seaman Sig Helland	35
The Riots of Newark Margaret Farrington	41
A Child's Prayer Lynn Assimacopoulos	45
Little Red Stomping Hood Keith Jensen	47
Amen Lynn Assimacopoulos	51

One-Room Country Schools   53

Teaching the Nontraditional Student   55
    Eunice & Howard Hovland

The All-Electric Farm   59
    Mary Thurman

Scout's Honor!   63
    Lynn Bethke

Boarding School Days   67
    B. Margaret Bankers

House Cleaning   71
    Robert Fedde

Pre-Cell Phone Ingenuity   73
    Nell Smith

My Playhouse   75
    Caroline Schoon

The Peppermint Bull   79
    Virgil Miller

It Takes a Community   83
    Jim Leffler

Escape From the City   90
    Lynn Assimacopoulos

The Car in the Cornfield   91
    Lynn Assimacopoulos

All Things Work Together for Good Arlette Villaume	93
The Hollyhocks Lynn Assimacopoulos	97
Royalty at the Lodge Mary Anderson	99
The Golden Harvest Mary George	103
Black, White or Gray Thomas Vanden Bosch	107
Only But Not Lonely Child Peryl Beckman	111
Grasshoppers Sylvia Fuoss	115
Sing Along With Mitch Audrey Jensen	121
To Market I Must Go Virginia Knorr	125
Raindrops Lynn Assimacopoulos	131
Embassy Tales Bon Slade	133
Concetta Connie McLauchlan	139

The Bride's First Donuts   143
   Alice Mikkelson

The Gypsy Woman   145
   Theresa Collins

Ms. Nightingale of the Plains   149
   Beulah Langenfeld

Beulah Langenfeld Day   153
   Beulah Langenfeld

A Hole for the Future   155
   Marilyn Peters

Answering My Country's Call   159
   Stan Lovro

Living the American Dream   163
   Ardeth Rang

?????   167
   Lynn Assimacopoulos

Elroy and Lois were married during World War II and many food items including sugar were rationed. The government issued each family a book with coupons for rationed items. When the coupons were gone for that item, the store would not sell them.

Lois wanted a wedding cake which required more sugar than the baker or Lois's family had. The word went out about Lois's plight and soon sugar arrived, $1/4^{th}$ cup at a time. On the day of the wedding, the beautifully decorated cake was shared by all the guests.

WORDS

Pastor Elroy Skaar

Pastor Elroy and his wife, Lois, moved to Prairie Creek in May of 2009. They have two children. The following poetry is found in Pastor's book *My Very Own Words*, with this explanation: On the following pages are my words, impressions of daily living, expressions from daily experiences, a philosophy forged by years. Pastor Skaar passed away in May 2009. Lois continues to live at Prairie Creek and is an inspiration to us all.

> If I were a cook I would bake a fine cake.
> If I were a potter I would mold a fine pot.
> If I were a jeweler I would shape a fine ring:
> > But my talent is found in words,
> > I mold them, I shape them,
> > I make them into sentences and paragraphs,
> > I write them and I speak them:
>
> Words of thanks, Words of praise,
> Words of admonition, Words of courage.
> I use words to express my thoughts,
> To convey ideas, feelings, moods.
> To instruct, to inspire, to give hope.

The Eitrheim family farm homesteaded in 1874. Because it is still owned by a family member, it is listed by the Historical Society as a Century Farm.

The future Reverend Norman Eitrheim, three years old, thinking: "My grandparents homesteaded here, my parents work the land today, and, someday it will all be mine!"

ROOTS INTO WINGS

Norm Eitrheim

After graduating from Augustana College, Norm graduated from Luther Seminary in St. Paul, MN. After serving two parishes, Norm was the Assistant to the President of Luther Seminary. He was the Bishop of the South Dakota Synod for 15 years. Norm and his wife, Clarice, have four children. They moved to Prairie Creek in 2007.

My maternal grandmother died during my freshman year in college. She had lived with my family all my growing up years. She was rich in stories about her incredible life. I heard those stories of her lifetime over and over, but as a kid, I wasn't really interested. Her insights, wisdom, and values shaped my life in profound ways. I would cherish some time with her now to record her stories with an audio or video recorder. Maybe that's why, at my age of 81 years, I have an interest in sharing and saving my stories for my children and grandchildren so that when I am gone, the inevitable fire of my death is not a threat to preserving my legacy.

My grandmother, Ann Opdahl Thompson, emigrated from Norway, at ten years of age, with her family during the Civil War. The voyage by sailing vessel took six weeks because a storm in the North Sea broke the mast and it needed to be repaired in Liverpool, England. A week of doldrums in the middle of the Atlantic meant more delay.

Food and water were short. One person died and was buried at sea; and a baby, Atlanta Maria, was born.

In 1874, Anna and her husband, Thorsten, and a two-week-old son, left from the Albert Lea, Minnesota area to homestead in Minnehaha County, northwest of Sioux Falls, Dakota Territory. The trip by covered wagon took two weeks. They arrived on July 2nd; it was too late to plant a crop and their garden was eaten by grasshoppers. My grandfather had planted tobacco plants, but the grasshoppers ate them. Do you know if grasshoppers spit? For shelter, these settlers dug a hole in the ground; both the walls and floor were not covered. My grandmother said it wasn't a problem if babies ate dirt since it was "clean" dirt. They lived in that dugout for four years until rats found a home in the ceiling and roof and my grandmother gave the ultimatum (and she was capable of that) that a house would be built. Since the railroad had not arrived in Sioux Falls, they hauled lumber 70 miles from Worthington, Minnesota, and built the small house where they raised twelve children. It also became the house where my parents, two brothers, a sister, my grandmother, and I lived.

I have deep roots in that homestead. The Thompson homestead was honored in 1976, for having descendants of the original homesteaders still living there. My father and mother bought that farm from my grandmother for $90 an acre in 1928, and made the last payment in 1939 when adjoining farms were selling for $35 an acre. My brother farmed the land for a few years until multiple sclerosis forced him to quit. My sister and her husband were the next owners and now their son, the fourth generation, lives there and has built a large dairy operation.

The one room country school provided a good education. I rode a pony, Patsy, the half mile to school, tied the reins around her neck and she ran home full speed. I had never seen a basketball game, so in eighth grade I rode

Patsy five miles into town to see a high school basketball game and, of course, rode home in the dark.

An open country Lutheran Church was the social, as well as, religious center for our family. The whole family went to Luther League and to Men's Brotherhood and the younger children went to Ladies' Aid with my mother. The big social event of the year was the Sioux Empire State Fair where we exhibited our 4-H "baby beef" calves. Trips to Sioux Falls were rare; one annual trip in August was to buy school supplies, including clothes, and the other was to buy Christmas gifts. Saturday night found our family in Dell Rapids where egg and cream money paid for groceries. During the summer we went to Baltic on Wednesday nights. Before daylight time made it too late, the merchants provided a free movie (often an "oater") that was projected on the exterior wall of one of the stores.

As a third generation of immigrant grandparents and the second generation of an immigrant father (my father at age 19 came to the United States alone without any family), I didn't learn Norwegian at home. My mother, a teacher, did not want her children learning English as a second language in first grade. Consequently, I am like nearly all third-generation descendants of immigrants from all non-English speaking countries who come to the U.S. They know only English. I regret that I am not bilingual.

Although I didn't know Norwegian, I heard the quaint ways in which they conversed in Baltic. Two farmers would meet in town in clean overalls, a plaid shirt, and a tie tucked under the overall bib, and one would say, "Are yew in town, too?" The response would be, "Yah, I gass so" or "Yah, I tink so." Tentative answers were typical of many Norwegian-Americans. Often, they would wonder rather than right-out know. They would come inside on a bitter winter day with ear-lappers and fogged glasses and say, "I vonder if it's cold out today?" Infinitives were often used to describe subjects. Instead of saying that someone eats too much, they would say, "Oh, he's so terrible to eat." Even compliments were expressed the same way. Instead of saying that Dagny is a good pianist, they would say, "Dagny is so good to play the piano." If there was a lull in conversation, Norwegians would often fill in the lull with a short inward breath enunciating the word "yup."

I am proud and grateful for my heritage. My roots gave me wings. I have had the opportunity to do things that a South Dakota farm boy would never dream about. I have been privileged to visit 49 of the 50 states and 5 of the 7 continents. I have shaken hands with both Pope John Paul and Pope Benedict; not many Lutherans have had that opportunity. I am deeply grateful for my roots in family, in the land, in the United States of America, and in communities of faith. I have been blessed with a goodly and a Godly heritage.

PRACTICING MEDICINE BEFORE CELL PHONES

Dr. Tom Ludgate

Dr. Tom and his wife, Ruth, moved into Prairie Creek in 2006. He practiced veterinary medicine in Moody County, South Dakota, from 1944 to 1969. Tom is a published author of a book, *The Prairie Practitioners*, in 1996, which is in the Library of Congress. Tom and Ruth are the parents of four children. Ruth's job was to track down her husband in emergencies and she agrees that cell phones would have been very helpful.

It was one of those winter nights on the South Dakota prairie when one went to bed wondering about the blizzard that started gaining strength about mid-afternoon. The forecast was for more snow and strong winds ending about noon tomorrow. It didn't sound too bad for the local veterinarian, who was thinking about some calls he could make tomorrow, maybe later in the afternoon if some of the roads were cleared by then.

The phone rang shortly before 2:00 a.m. It was one of his clients who lived about 15 miles northeast of town. It seems one of his cows needed attention as soon as possible. He apologized and explained he had done everything he knew how to do, but the cow was in pretty bad shape and could Doc come out right away? I said I would try.

The good doctor's wife sat up in bed with a quizzical look. "Oh! Please don't go out there on a night like this. Come back to bed."

"Oh, I have to go. If I start not showing up when I am needed, what will that do to my practice? And Fred Wende is a good guy, a good farmer, friend and client. I've got to go!"

The fifteen miles out to the farm was on township roads covered with a layer of gravel. Travel was slow with poor visibility and I needed to buck some snow that was drifting here and there across the road.

On the way out to the farm, I knew what needed to be done with Fred's cow. She had just calved and I was pretty sure it was hypocalcaemia and that the treatment would involve intravenously feeding calcium glucomate to the cow as soon as possible; failure to do so would mean a quick death.

I was expecting to see some light from the house as I pulled into the driveway. The barn was also dark. I decided to park as close to the house as I could and blast my horn. No lights; no response. After a few repeated honks, a light appeared and then several more. Fred came to the door and yelled, "What the *?@#%&* do you want?"

"I came to work on your cow. This is Dr. Tom, you called earlier."

"I called? I wouldn't expect anybody to come out on a night like this, even for a very valuable cow."

"Sorry for getting you up on a night like this. I did receive a call and I thought it was you." I knew how he felt having to get up on a night like this!

I turned around and headed for the road as I wondered what to do. It came to me that maybe I misunderstood the name. I had another client by the name of Fred Wenge. The two names were similar and as I remembered the urgency of his call, I decided to try to help him out.

As bad luck would have it, I needed to go back to town and then go another nine miles, this time south of town. More roads, still dark and snowing, but maybe the wind was letting up a little, I said out loud, hoping to convince myself that there might be something good about the blizzard.

There was light in the barn so I grabbed my bag and let myself in. The farmer was working with the cow and looked a little short of patience. "What took you so long? I was beginning to think that you weren't coming," he said, a little put out, but added, "I am glad to see you. I hope it is not too late for Bessie here. You can see she is one valuable cow."

I did a few preliminary observations, but I knew what I had to do. The IV went well and after a short visit, I wished the farmer and his cow the best of luck and collected my $10 fee. And I was on the road again.

As I drove into my driveway, I noticed day was breaking with some first light coming out of the east. I was looking forward to a warm bed and maybe a couple hours of sleep.

My wife awakened and was happy to see me. "I was so worried and got up a couple of times to look out the window. That wind was still howling and the snow was coming down even faster than the last time I looked. I will go to the kitchen and cook up some coffee and make a little to eat," she said as she started to get out of bed.

"Thanks, but a warm bed looks better to me right now." I crawled into bed as my dear wife asked over her shoulder, "So, how did it go? Were there any problems?"

"Nah, it was fine," I mumbled. "In the last four hours, I've plowed about 35 miles of snow-covered roads in the middle of a blizzard, made two clients angry and collected a $10 service call. I'm tired and cold, but I am satisfied I did the best I could."

 The cell phone would have been useful in getting emergency phone calls to Doc.

FOLLOW THE PIPER

After WWI, there were four veterinarians in Moody County treating farm animals. Today, there are no rural veterinarians living there. The services Dr. Tom delivered are now history.

In 1944, there were two or three farms on one section of good farmland. Each farm commonly raised beef, dairy, hogs, and chickens. Crop farms today need to be much larger to be profitable and are void of animals. Livestock farms are planned to raise one type of animal. Veterinary clinics provide needed services.

GRANDPA'S CHRISTMAS CABOOSE

Rocky Ryan

Gerald (Rocky) Ryan has a storehouse of stories that cover more than 84 years of life experience. One of his favorite collections of the Great Depression is of traveling over the river and through the woods to his Grandmother's house. Rocky and his wife, Judy, moved to Prairie Creek in 2010. They have two children and three grandchildren.

During the Roaring Twenties, my father and his younger brother shared ownership in a Dodge touring car. Dad and Mom drove that car for almost ten years after they were married, until all three of us kids were born. We lived in Grand Forks, North Dakota, while my mom's folks lived in Roseau, Minnesota, more than 140 miles away. It was a long trip to take in a ragtop.

During the Christmas holidays, Mom would bundle us into long wool underwear, warm ribbed-wool stockings, snow pants, leather shoes, hand-knit sweaters, sheepskin coats, caps with leathery flaps, scarves and flat, scratchy mittens.

Dad would heat bricks in the stove, bundle them into burlap sacks and pack them between me and my brother in the back seat. Mom would put Sister and our lunch in her lap in the front seat and we'd set out on our journey.

We'd ride for what seemed like forever. Finally, the livery stable on the edge of Roseau would come into view.

Dad would drive the roadster into the livery, park the car and Grandpa Pete would come around the corner in the Christmas Caboose.

The caboose was a big wooden box Grandpa had built on a flat bed bolted to a horse-drawn sleigh. It looked something like an ice shack. It was taller than Grandpa when he stood on the ground, but Grandpa and our folks had to crouch in order to get through the back door. We kids could stand straight up and walk inside.

Pat and Mike, Grandpa's team of big dark brown Belgian workhorses, pulled the sleigh. Grandpa had cut two holes in the front of the caboose for their reins. He drove from inside, sitting on one of the benches he'd built along the sides of the caboose.

A kerosene-burning stove with a metal top sat in the middle of the shack's floor. It gave off a lot of heat, a little smoke, and a bad smell. Grandpa had cut small windows on either side of the caboose and covered them with isinglass. The windows were just big enough to let a little light in and draw the smoke and smell out.

Grandpa and Grandma's farmstead was about seven miles northwest, on the Canadian border. In the winter, there was a lot of snow up there, and no snowplows. Without access to the roads, Grandpa had to drive the horses and caboose over the river, through the woods and across the fields.

It took more than two hours to get to the farmstead, but Pat and Mike knew the way. Grandpa would give the big horses a tap with the reins and give them their head. They'd pull our Christmas caboose through the town of Roseau, down onto the ice-covered Roseau River and slide the caboose along the ice on the river all the way to the Dines' farm. Then, they'd pull us up and out of the riverbed and take up a steady pace west, over the woods and fields, toward home and the barn.

Mom and Dad, my brother, sister and I would sit curled up on the benches around the heater, covered in blankets. Grandpa would keep us all going by telling stories, singing songs and giving us cold milk to drink with Mother's lunch.

We boys would stare out the isinglass windows until we'd nod off to sleep. As we got closer to home, Pat and Mike would pick up the pace and we'd begin to stir.

Grandpa would whisper, "Wake up, boys. We're almost there. Watch for the candles Grandma has put in the windows! Which of you will be the first to see them?"

We'd rub our eyes, tumble off the benches and snub our noses against the windows. Pretty soon, Grandma's candles would blink into view. My brother and I would holler, "I see them! I see Grandma's candles!" and squabble over who saw them first.

Pat and Mike would slow their pace and their big hooves would squeak to a stop at the front door. While Grandpa took Pat and Mike into the barn to curry and feed them, we'd crawl out of the caboose and into Grandma's warm kitchen.

After hugs all around, Grandma would begin to light what seemed like hundreds of tiny candles on the Christmas tree. Grandpa would come in from the barn and we'd all sit down for our Christmas Eve supper of lutefisk and lefse.

Many of my memories have begun to fade. I dimly remember Christmas services, handmade presents, visits with relatives, the crust of ice that froze over the pitcher of drinking water in the bedroom during the night, the sound of Grandma shaking grates in the woodstove when it was time to get up, and eating cold potatoes and fish with Grandpa before going out to do chores.

But my memories of our journeys in Grandpa's Christmas caboose are still as crisp and new as the snow on the ice of the Roseau River.

I thought my grandparents must be rich, indeed. They had a big, warm house, a barn, horses, a Christmas tree and all sorts of good things to eat. Much later, I learned they had an annual income of around $300.

THE CAT FROM SOUTHSIDE CHICAGO

Mick Pickford

Grandpa looked at his newborn grandson and declared that he looked like a "Mick." By the time he entered college, he stood 5'6" and weighed 175 pounds. His love for wrestling and football caused him to play beyond his stature. Mick and his wife were married for 48 years and had five children. He moved into Prairie Creek in May of 2010

Although I thought growing up in Southside Chicago was great, something inside of me was aching to get out of the neighborhood. I liked the little ethnic communities surrounding our house and some excitement and adventure could always be found.

I hoped my athletic abilities would be the ticket out. The neighboring high school had an outstanding football team and scholarships weren't unusual. Using the address of my grandparent's house, I became a student there.

I went out for football and wrestling. Wrestling was assigned by weight classes, but in football I wasn't so lucky. Since I wanted to be on the line, I had to prove to the coach I could handle the big guys. My goal of getting a scholarship to attend Morningside College in Sioux City, Iowa, was achieved.

By that time, the other guys were bigger and tougher. My only choice was to get tougher. I held my own until I played too hard and injuries came along. I never finished a

FOLLOW THE PIPER

season trying to beat the other guy and had to sit out the rest of the season.

It all lead to a career I loved. For 48 years, I coached football and wrestling in Iowa, and also did some refereeing. Twice I took some wrestlers to the Olympics in Europe and Los Angeles.

My claim to fame, however, was my uncanny ability to get hit by cars; nine times, same as cats get! I don't consider myself careless; just unlucky dodging cars. None of the accidents resulted in any broken bones, but each time I was taken to a medical facility to have my scrapes and bruises checked out. It all started at an early age and continued for many years.

*When I was four, my mother asked me to run across the street to the market. Mom stood on the stoop to watch me cross. One car stopped and she waved me across. While that car stopped, the next one didn't. I went under the car, but avoided the tires, kinda like what happens to dogs.

*Two years later, I took my brother's bike to visit friends. On the return trip, I went through the schoolyard onto a gravel road. That car hit me and threw me 20 feet into the air.

*In fifth grade, I was on my bike and went through an alley. A car hit me and I was in the air again!

*In junior high, I was on my bike, on my way to visit a girl and cut through the florist's parking lot. I landed in a grassy ditch and never got to see the girl.

*I went to a movie and took the streetcar home. Stepping off the front of the streetcar, a car hit me before my foot touched Mother Earth. I flew forward and the driver took me home.

*Again, I went to a movie on my bike and was clipped from behind. The driver stopped, picked me and my broken bike up, and took us home.

*One day, my wife and I were depositing a check in a Sioux City bank. A car came around the corner, and as I pushed my wife out of the way, I got clipped again. This time, I saw the car coming.

*At the Wisconsin Dells, we were watching a parade. I heard a car coming in time to again push my wife out of the way, but I got smacked. I never did figure out where that car came from.

*Our family was trying to go through a parade to get to the other side. Our car stalled and I got out to push it out of the way of the parade. My wife was helping push when a car came along. I pushed her out of the way so she wouldn't get pinned. I got pinned!

Now in my late seventies, I hope for better luck. Last year, however, I fell face forward, stumbling over a cracked sidewalk. The "horn" on the top of my head grew to be about three inches tall and it has taken about a year to dissolve. Presently, my left shoulder is in a mechanical sling due to another fall in which I broke three bones in my elbow, and I'm spending time in physical therapy rehab.

Maybe I don't mend as fast as I did in college, but I still mend! And, I'm trying to be more careful than I was in the past.

Bigger doesn't make him better. You are quicker and stronger; now, let's see if you are smarter? Go get him, shorty!

A NORWEGIAN SEAMAN

Sig Helland

Sig moved to Minnesota and started by remodeling homes; he then built new homes, then built a lumberyard and cabinet shop. He was known for building cabinets. His wife, Anne, was the bookkeeper. They had a "pigeon pair" family, a boy and a girl. Sig retired in 1982, and they spent 22 winters on South Padre Island, Texas on the Mexican Gulf. They moved to Brandon, then to Sioux Falls in 2000, and to Prairie Creek in 2008.

As a poor young lad from Olen, Norway, I was unable to find work during the Depression of the '30s. So, at the age of 16, I decided to join the Norwegian Merchant Marines and got a job on a commercial ship. Little did I know that for the next 13 years I would be spending most of my life at sea on oil tankers and cargo ships.

On June 11, 1940, it was a beautiful night on the Mediterranean Sea. All of a sudden, about eleven o'clock, our ship was torpedoed by an Italian submarine. I was an AB Seaman on this ship and one of the blessed ones to escape death by scurrying to one of the lifeboats. Many others were not so fortunate. Then came the second torpedo, which went right through the engine room. All I could hear was the Captain yelling out, "Get down" and "Man the lifeboats."

Shortly after the ship sank and disappeared into the Mediterranean Sea, the lifeboats got close together and the

Captain called out our names to record the number of survivors. Eight men were killed that night.

We were in bad shape, but soon we spotted a ship with all its lights on. The Captain signaled for help by Morse Code with his flashlight. He learned this ship was going to Spain, but he did not want to go because of the danger. He wanted to go to Egypt. Seamen always try to help anyone in need so the Spanish Captain said, "We will get as close as possible to you, you all come on board and you can stay until daylight." The wounded were taken into the Spanish Captain's salon and cared for as best they could. The Spanish steward and cook were ordered to the galley by their Captain to cook breakfast for us. We had bacon, eggs and fresh bread. It tasted so good!

After daylight, aboard the Spanish ship, we started crisscrossing the debris in the ocean left behind by our ship and the lifeboats, searching for survivors, but none were found. We sailed toward Egypt and when we arrived in Alexandria, our wounded were taken to the hospital and the rest of us were taken to an English seaman's home. He let the officers have beds and the rest of us had mats on a cement floor. In port, the crew from the British ship gathered all their football uniforms and gave them to us to wear. Our clothes were soaked with oil.

The next morning, our Captain went to the Norwegian Consulate and saw the Vice Consul, but he was hesitant to help as he did not want to be left with the bill. A Norwegian judge living in Alexandria visited us and advocated on our behalf. He went to the Consulate and told him that the Norwegian government was now located in London and, by law, he had to help us. On the second day, we were taken to a men's store, allowed to buy anything we wanted, and put it on the Norwegian government's tab. We were sent to a very nice hotel located on a beautiful Mediterranean beach, where we stayed for two weeks.

I was wondering where my next check was coming from and the answer came the next day when the British Navy brought in an Italian passenger ship. Many of us signed on as crew. We sailed to different ports in the Mediterranean Middle East. On the return trip from Port Said, I came down with a severe ear infection and was sent to a hospital. By the time I was discharged, my ship had set sail.

The Norwegian Consulate then assigned me to a big Norwegian oil tanker that brought supplies, oil, and gas to the Island of Malta, which was used by Britain as one of their large military bases. For this reason, it was a dangerous journey as we sailed close to Italy. The waters were full of submarines and many enemy planes flew overhead. The British Admiral called us the "Suicide Flotilla." The biggest and worse battle I remember was in Malta. We were bombed mercilessly. After the all clear signal, the British harbor patrol boats would go out to pick up downed German pilots and bring them back as prisoners. Often, as the British brought the Germans back to shore, the women of Malta, who were so angry with the Germans, would try to attack them with butcher knives. They had to increase the number of security guards. After the terrible battles, some small towns had nothing left but rubble; a ghost town left standing.

At this same time, Germans advanced swiftly across Greece. General Rommel was rapidly advancing across North Africa so we could not go through the Suez Canal. Thus, we went west to Gibraltar. We sailed very close to the North African coast between Cape Bon and the Island of Panelleria. I was on watch that night. It was a beautiful clear sky with stars shining and we could see the huge shadow of the island occupied by the Germans. I heard what I thought was thunder, but knew that was not possible on such a clear night. It turned out to be the sound of a fierce battle between the British and Italian Navies. The next morning I could see an Italian plane circling above us.

We were spotted even though our ship was camouflaged. By 1:00 p.m., they started to bomb us. Fortunately, we had one anti aircraft gun on board and kept it going so they could not just drop a bomb down the funnel. Again, I heard "Man the guns" and "Stay under cover." We went zigzagging, but never got hit. However, there was a lot of shrapnel that landed on our deck.

When bombing started, we sailed from Malta with a British ship, but it sailed quickly and left us behind. As evening fell, the Italian or German planes came again, dropping torpedoes. We reversed the engine and went full speed, turned starboard, but were unable to avoid two torpedoes that hit our ship. We ordered steam into every tank, which came out through the hatches. The Germans assumed we were on fire. Later, we realized our ship had a hole big enough to drive a bus through. We "limped" into Gibraltar during the night and the next morning were surrounded by the British Navy, which had come from a battle in the Mediterranean Sea. They had just successfully sunk a lot of Italian warships.

We anchored in the Bay of Gibraltar as we couldn't get into dry dock to repair the ship. We hired Spanish workers and they were able to close the hole with steel rods and cement. Within two weeks we were seaworthy and able to travel. Unfortunately for us, just as we set sail, a 35,000 ton British battleship named the "Warspite" sailed into the Bay of Gibraltar, lost their steering and was headed right towards our ship. The crash cut a 60' long hole in this ship that had just been repaired. So, back into the dockyard for two more weeks of repair. We maintained our duties, but also got time off to enjoy ourselves. We studied in the library, went to dances, drank beer and went up into the mountains to be entertained by the monkeys. While in Gibraltar, I went to gunner school and learned how to man the guns.

Our next order was to sail all alone to Galveston, Texas, for further repairs. After living in the darkness for so long, seeing a city all lit up was a real treat. We spent about a month there and had a great time that summer doing what seamen do...enjoying the nightlife and swimming. We were sent to Houston, Texas, to load up with oil and head back to England. We sailed along the coast of New York to Halifax, Nova Scotia. We formed convoys to cross the ocean and harbored in Scapa Flow on the Orkney Islands.

I left the ship early in 1942, and went to London to navigation school. There was always a lot of bombing in London, but I refused to go to an air raid shelter knowing I wouldn't die before my name was called. After finishing navigation school, I went back to sea again as an officer and ended up second in command of a ship. We were in France when on May 8, 1945, the war ended. What a lot of celebrating!

I went back to London and worked for the Norwegian Shipping and Trade Mission until 1946, and then returned to Norway, where I attended carpentry school to learn architecture, drafting, estimating, and home building. By this time, I had married Anne and needed to earn a living, so I went to sea again, sailing a cargo/passenger ship from New York along the east coast of Maine to the Caribbean to Buenos Aires, Argentina, and back again. When I returned after two years, my two and one-half year old son did not know me. It was time to give up sailing. Anne and I took all the money we had saved and headed for the United States, the "land of golden opportunity" and ended up in Blue Earth, Minnesota.

 When Sig and Anne moved back to Norway, Anne learned the Norwegian language and spoke it with a British accent.

THE RIOTS OF NEWARK

Margaret Farrington

Margaret spent most of her professional life in Newark, NJ. She retired from Aetna Life & Casualty in 1987, and moved to Sioux Falls. Margaret lives to volunteer; it gives purpose to her life. She was a mentor at Eugene Field Elementary and the Children's Home Society. Margaret moved to Prairie Creek in April 2007, and continues to volunteer when she is able.

I grew up in Wheaton, Illinois, and later moved to Newark, New Jersey, when my father took a position with ITT. In 1945, I was awarded a Presidential Scholarship from the University of Dubuque in Iowa, where I majored in Political Science and English. I worked hard academically as well as physically. In the mornings I worked in the library in the shelving department, at noon I worked in the commons, and at night I monitored in the library. After three and one-half years, I graduated in 1949.

My first job interview was one that still makes me smile. It was in East Orange, New Jersey, with Liberty Mutual Insurance Company, in the claims department. I wore a navy blue pinstriped suit with high heels, a white hat and white gloves. My hair was just so and everything matched. I was the properly dressed businesswoman of the '50s and proud of it. I got the job and worked there for a while. I knew it was a man's world at this time, but I was determined to prove that I could compete with any of them even though women were never given a salary as large as a man's for the same position. I worked for Liberty Mutual for eight years.

In 1954, I quit my job and married Michael G. Farrington. My husband inherited some cottages at Cape Cod, Massachusetts, so we moved there. Living at Cape Cod was not a pleasant experience and it was very stressful on our marriage, which soon ended in 1961.

Then I moved to Newark, New Jersey, and decided to apply for a position with Aetna Life and Casualty Insurance as an underwriter. For that interview, I wore the same navy blue pinstriped suit, with high heels, and the same hat and white gloves. I was offered the job and soon learned it was a challenge. I loved this job and worked as a liaison between the independent agents who represented Aetna and such companies as Johnson & Johnson and other high-profile names. Because of the account of Johnson & Johnson, I was given access to Lloyd's of London. It was a very memorable time when I took my father with me to London to visit Lloyd's of London. To see his excitement on this trip was something I will always cherish.

I enjoyed going to work every day, but on a certain Thursday night during the summer of 1967, the race riots took place in Newark. This was, and still is, a poor city with many people living below the poverty level. There was a lot of unrest especially at the time the riots broke out in Watts, California. Our office was located near a poorer section of the city, but not far from Seton Hall University. I usually took the bus to work and that morning we were told there was trouble in our section of the city and that we were not to look at anyone or make eye contact with anyone on the street. I pretended to read a book on the bus and all the way into my office. When the bus stopped, we saw armored personnel carriers on every corner. There were policemen, the National Guardsmen, and U. S. Army soldiers all over the place. They were trying to protect the banks as the mob was shouting, "We want money." All banks and businesses were closed at this time. It was wild and noisy and scary.

We were sent home at noon, but the buses would not run so we had to have the Army personnel escort us by foot to the train station, which was one-fourth mile away. On the other end of the train ride, I had to walk three miles to get home as I lived close to South Orange, New Jersey.

For several nightmarish nights, I could envision the rioters screaming and shouting slurs and obscenities. They threw rocks or anything they could pick up, and tipped over cars and set them on fire. They set buildings on fire as well. There was a lot of looting. The liquor stores were looted the most and then the appliance and furniture stores, but no business escaped the looting. Most of that section of town was burned down. The total scene was worse than a horror movie, but I never did hear that anyone was killed during this time. It all seemed so surreal.

The businesses, including my office, stayed closed for four days, from Thursday until Tuesday. The Army had managed to keep the riots away from the nearby university and from spreading to our office or to the principle stores that were located downtown. The policemen could not do such a job without the help of the Army and the National Guard. For a long time, there was a curfew from 10:00 p.m. to 6:00 a.m.

Not knowing that the riots were still going strong on the following Monday, I took the bus to work that morning. But, as we arrived there, we knew we were in trouble. When the bus stopped, someone threw a tear gas canister into the bus. Everyone screamed and shoved others so they could get outside as quickly as possible, and gasped to get their breath. The burning in the lungs and the coughing were very painful. Our eyes burned mercilessly and we became nauseous. It was a mess! Again, we were escorted out of the area, but as we were leaving, we could still hear all those men shouting. I did not see any women among the riots. By

Wednesday, most of the town was returning to normal, but with many bad memories.

By 1987, the city still looked like it had been hit by bombs. Sections of whole neighborhoods had not been rebuilt. No one seemed to know just why they had rioted. The city was in poverty and unemployment was high but they destroyed so many of their own homes and businesses and left the place in ruins. They gained nothing and there still seemed to be no incentive to improve their living quarters. The only thing I hear now is that they have been given government grants for education. Hopefully, that will help to direct the restless youth.

 It was possible for a woman to be successful in the corporate world as early as the 1950s.

A CHILD'S PRAYER

Lynn Assimacopoulos

Lynn graduated from the University of Minnesota, with a Bachelor of Nursing degree. She and her husband provided medical care in Minnesota, California, Nebraska and South Dakota. Lynn is a published author of *I Thought There Was A Road There*, a delightful book about raising their three boys. She moved to Prairie Creek in 2008.

When I was around seven years old, my mother told me to come in from playing outside. I really did not want to. Then, she told me to go to bed and remember to say my usual "Now I lay me down to sleep" prayer. I was angry so I decided to make up my own prayer.

I sleep by night
I play by day
But Jesus always leads my way.

I do not cry
I do not fear
For Jesus is always very near.

We should praise Jesus
Every day
For He is waiting to light our way.

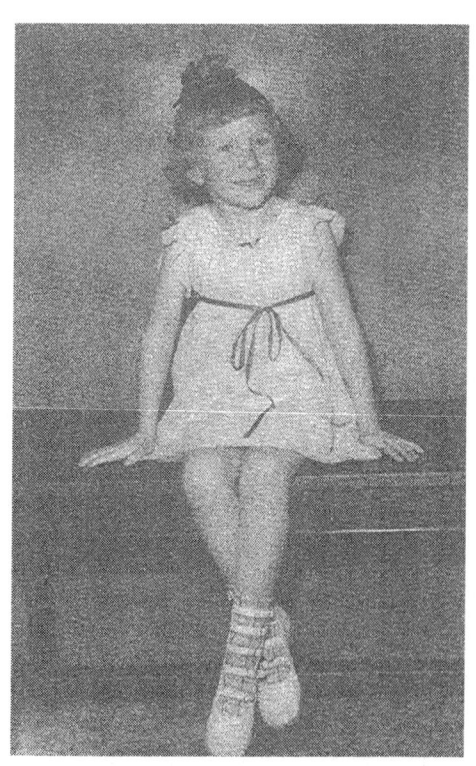

Li'l Red Stomping Hood

LITTLE RED STOMPING HOOD

Keith Jensen

Keith and his wife, Audrey, the "Stomper," moved into the Lodge in 2008. They raised six boys and moved seven times in five different upper Midwest states. Keith spent 43 years in education. Currently, none of the boys are in jail!

If one were familiar with southeast South Dakota and carefully placed one's thumb over a certain area on a decent-sized South Dakota map, one could pretty much cover that area known as Little Denmark. In that area, one would find a number of churches, lots of country schools and a couple of country towns. In 1941, my family and I lived on a farm towards the southern part of Little Denmark. Our lives revolved around two institutions a mile apart; both played a huge part in our lives although they were very different and very much alike.

Our one room schoolhouse fit in well with the sparseness of the prairie. The building itself was quite small, no basement, a small room for coats and overshoes, and a classroom; but it was larger than the other building on the one acre lot: the outhouse. A coal stove provided heat while a piece of tin surrounded the stove for a purpose I never did figure out. A teacher's desk, 20 student desks, and a piano sat inside the room.

The church was in the style of the other country churches, white siding, a very tall bell tower, a generous entry, beautiful windows, the worship area and a balcony. The basement held a generous number of people for wedding receptions, silver and golden wedding parties, special church festivals and funerals. The cemetery surrounded the church. The outhouse was behind the church where the Christians could maintain a fair amount of modesty when nature made the visit necessary.

The school was open eight months of the year to fit the rhythm of the farm families. All of our classmates had last names ending in "sen": Christensen, Sorensen, Jensen, Swensen and Larsen. Many of the same families attended the church, but other Danish families brought new names like Storgaard, Tanderuup and Fastruup. But, we were still 100% Danish.

The big event each year at school was the Christmas program. Country schoolteachers knew that their competence was often determined by the quality of the program. So, it only seemed necessary to take an inordinate number of school days to practice for the program. We practiced speaking clearly and loudly, working out every detail to perfection. The program had to be perfect.

The fathers came in several weeks in advance of the program to build a small stage at the front of the room. Wires were strung and sheets were hung so the main stage would have curtains that opened and closed just like on Broadway. The girls had a private area stage left and the boys shared their privacy with the coal stove on stage right.

On the night of the performance, the student desks were pushed to the east and west sides where the little brothers and sisters could sit along with friends and cousins. The mothers sat in the middle and the fathers stood in the back. With the room packed and the windows decorated, the dim lantern that hung from the ceiling helped hide the bareness of the room.

World War II was in full swing so it wasn't a surprise when our teacher picked out plays dealing with the war and war songs were sung to honor the neighbor boys who were in the military. My brother, four years older than I, got the idea during the performance that the play would be more realistic for the guests if he used his rhythm stick to strike the tin surrounding the stove making it sound like bombs were falling. He was so impressed that the bombs began to fall faster and louder. Once the teacher figured out where the racket was coming from, she made an emergency visit to stage left to end the sound effects. This she did with a simple thumb tap to his head, which ended the noisiest bomb attack of World War II. She was also unimpressed when he chose to deliver the punch line of the play in Danish, but it was too late to remedy that piece of creativity. After all, she was protecting her credentials for future employment.

The church Christmas program was directed by the Sunday school teachers, the mothers of the church. The programs were historical and it was predictable that some of the younger students would make errors and have memory lapses that added to the charm of the program. The congregation never got tired of seeing this year's Mary rocking the baby Jesus while Joseph, in his father's bathrobe, stood watch. Shepherds, Wise Men and angels appeared to tell the glorious story.

Our church was the most beautiful building I had ever seen, especially the interior on Christmas night. The altar consisted of many spires pointing to heaven itself, while a beautiful life-sized statue of Christ stood in the middle. At night when we performed our program, the high ceilings created little corners of blackness where the lamps that stood on beautiful sconces lit up the colorful windows made of colored glass and etched designs. The Christmas tree stood just inside the communion railing. On the other side of the room stood the pulpit, which our minister entered by climbing five steps to lead his faithful flock on high. The pump organ moaned ethereal notes clear up to the balcony. The pews easily held the Christmas guests.

But something entirely unexpected happened toward the end of the program. The parishioners were farm families with the exception of the family from town, who had a girl Sunday school age. Because the family found it difficult to travel the distance, church attendance was irregular and we children were unfamiliar with this little girl, who was listed on the program as singing a solo. It was with some curiosity that we watched her come forward for her part in the program. Something happened toward the middle of the solo that irritated this little red-haired girl and caused her to stomp her foot, point her finger at us and declare in a loud voice, "I won't, I won't, I won't sing one more word," and stomp back to sit by her mother. We were bewildered as to what prompted this behavior, although our teacher accused us of behaving badly, which caused this little spitfire to assume we were making fun of her. But I was smitten and this little whippersnapper became my wife thirteen years later.

Before we were dismissed at the end of the program, our teachers, our mothers, questioned our behavior. The girls looked our way in a very accusing way. When the quiet became too much for me, I reminded them that I was one of the angels and without blame, but I did observe some Shepherds poking Joseph.

Nevertheless, we received our favorite Christmas treat of the year; a brown sack with an apple and an orange, some ribbon candy and lots of peanuts in the shell.

 Religion and education were two highly regarded values.

AMEN

Lynn Assimacopoulos

I drank my coffee
And burned my tongue
One thought I thought
As I sat.
Morning comes but once a day
I'm grateful
For just that!!!

ONE-ROOM COUNTRY SCHOOLS

When South Dakota became a state in 1889, the Federal government granted the state over 36 million acres. In each township, sections 16 and 36 were to be used for schools and other public purposes. If these lands were either sold or leased, the proceeds were deposited in permanent trust funds for education. Interest from the funds was to be used for funding education.

One-room schools were frequently built on land given by the farmer in the middle of each township so students could easily walk to school.

Teachers commonly boarded with farmers near the school. The teacher was in charge of things, including starting a fire in a pot-bellied stove. Students sitting near the stove were often too hot, while the others were cold. Restrooms were "outhouses" and drinking water was brought in from an outside pump.

Many teachers were educated by taking courses in the summer to prepare them to teach the three R's: Reading, Writing, and "Rithmatic."

Often 20 to 25 students in grades one through eight were taught by one teacher.

TEACHING THE NONTRADITIONAL STUDENT

Eunice & Howard Hovland

Eunice & Howard have worked as a team providing educational opportunities to students who have somehow missed the opportunity to learn the traditional way. In addition to teaching, they have conducted many workshops in South Dakota and other Midwest states. They earned Master's and many other education credits through the years. They moved to Prairie Creek in 2010.

Dr. Paul McKee's educational philosophy states, "See a need and teach to that need—it is when a man seeks knowledge of his own accord that his/her real education begins."

Consider that all adults come to an educational institution with an abundance of experiences and skills, however acquired, achievements, understandings, talents, capabilities. Or, on the other hand, with deficiencies, styles of learning, handicaps (physical and perhaps mental), and put them in a single class to upgrade their basic skills is really unreal.

One only needs to understand that students came for a purpose and their needs were apparently not being met. The fundamental secret of success is that INDIVIDUALIZATION is justified. No one needs to be in a classroom situation listening and doing work which is in their mind's eye as being boring, repetitive, waiting for someone else to catch up, too slow, or over their head. The individual approach may seem to be an expensive procedure. However, when one considers the alternatives, individualized instruction is a bargain.

Securing the GED (General Education Development) often becomes a fundamental step to those adults who did not secure a high school diploma.

Reasons for failing to get a diploma vary with each student. Here are a few: physical/mental limitations, poverty, needed at home, parental value system, distance to school, weather, teacher ridicule, poor grades, lack of interest, incompetent teachers. A GED is a critical step for basic employment or advancement.

One evening I straight-out asked one student, "Why do you want to learn how to read?" He shared that he wanted to get a better job. I pushed the conversation by asking "Why do you want to learn how to read?" He said he was a janitor and wanted to know how to read the labels on his cleaning supplies. I could see he wanted to tell me more.

Finally, he said he couldn't stand it anymore. With a sadness, he shared, "I can't stand it when my two little boys come home from Sunday school classes and crawl up on my knees and say, 'Daddy, read to me.'" He paused and repeated it again, only softer, "Daddy, read to me."

Another student came to me and asked, "What kind of alphabet do they use to write all of those books?" as he pointed to the many racks with books on the shelves.

"All of those books are written using the same alphabet, which we wanted you to study last night." He was astonished and quickly went over to his buddy to tell him. Neither one knew the alphabet nor could they read.

Under Title IIB, 44 million dollars was made available to the State Department of Education to operate ABE (Adult Basic Education) classes for two years. Ultimately, the bill helped many more individuals to take GED classes leading to many more happy and productive lives. It has proven to be a great investment, not only in personal lives, but to our economy.

 People deserve a second chance to become literate and to upgrade their basic skills.

This is the house . . .

    That has the kitchen . . .

        That has the table . . .

            On which Mary was born!

THE ALL-ELECTRIC FARM

Mary Thurman

Mary's mother was quite short and ready for delivery. The doctor advised her father to boil some water and put his wife on something very firm. With the help of his wife's sister, he chose to put his wife on the kitchen table where the little girl was born. Mary was a mischievous little girl, loved the farm, married and had four children of her own. She moved to Prairie Creek in 2008.

Emery and Gazena were married in 1921, and started farming in Lincoln County, South Dakota. Their first farm had a very small house with the only heat being a cook stove that burned cobs and wood. It was there that Mary Lorraine was delivered, on the kitchen table, on February 12, 1923.

I was their only child and Mother often called me a rascal. At two years of age, I was playing by the hog fence and fell into the pig yard. An old sow came racing toward me and the dog saved my life until Father could get to me. When I was four, I was declared lost. After a long hunt, they found me locked in the chicken house. The door was closed and the ammonia fumes were so strong I had to throw up.

My parents gave up church attendance for a while because their little girl was all over, wanting to sit on everybody's lap. Mother's father wondered why they weren't going to church. She told him, "We are too

FOLLOW THE PIPER

embarrassed to go because Mary makes too much commotion during the sermon."

In 1927, when I was four, Mother told me that we were moving to a farm close to Sioux Falls. Through the bank, Father was asked to build an all-electric farm, the first in South Dakota. A wealthy man and the banker had picked him to be the one to build it.

When the original farm buildings were torn down, it was decided to hire five carpenters from Sweden to start building. My mother's job was to make morning lunch, dinner, and afternoon lunch. We lived in the old house while they made a concrete basement with a Delco plant to supply electricity for the new house. Electricians, plumbers and other workers came to help and Mother was kept very busy. The kitchen was moved to the new concrete hog house while the big house was being finished. Gazena was able to hire a few hours of help to feed the hungry crew. The two women made lots of doughnuts, bread, pies, meat, potatoes and vegetables. The men loved her cooking, especially her gravy, one talent I acquired.

While all this was going on, Father was busy going on trips to buy cattle and getting the half section of land ready for crops and feedlots. With all the fencing and other chores, it seemed like there was no time to rest. Our families thought it was too much for them to do, but we did it: the first all-electric farm in South Dakota.

Mother continued to raise chickens; 500 at a time, and I would go with her to the hatchery to pick them up. The hens would lay eggs and the roosters were butchered for meat. Mother had a route where she could sell eggs, cream and meat. I loved riding along with my mother.

In 1928, the John Deere dealer visited Father and wanted him to plant at least sixty acres of corn and oats or barley. He said he would give Dad a good deal on the first complete John Deere farm tractor, planter, plow, and other farm implements.

Rocks needed to be removed from farm land. Some could be removed by using a stone boat, but other rocks needed to be blasted out of the ground. I loved going along, riding on the stone boat and watching the dynamite explode.

When the barn was finished, the men built the elevator, which was the first one of its kind. They wanted it to be rat free, so it was made of concrete. The wagons were hoisted up so the grain could be easily unloaded and put in bins. By this time, a second Delco plant was built to help run all the electricity. Many farmers came to see how we were farming.

There were fun times, too, as the workmen enjoyed playing tricks on one another. Sometimes they would give me a hammer or saw and tell me to go hide it. My favorite place would be a deep trench being dug for water pipes. They would pay me with candy bars. I was a rascal as a little girl, but, hopefully, I am better as an adult!!

Most farms didn't have electricity until REA (Rural Electric Association) became active in the mid-1940s, some 30 years later.

SCOUT'S HONOR!

Lynn Bethke

Lynn moved to Prairie Creek Lodge in September 2009. She worked in state government for 30 years retiring in 2001. She now works part-time at her church. Lynn has three children, three stepchildren, five grandchildren, nine step-grandchildren, and five step-greats!

My memories of being a Girl Scout in Troop 176 in Milwaukee, Wisconsin, are of the camaraderie and lasting friendships forged during this phase of my girlhood. I believe being a Girl Scout created in me the awareness and satisfaction of giving, of being in service to others that is still alive today.

Occasionally I come across the sash of fourteen proficiency badges I earned, the purpose of which were to show that a girl was prepared to use what she had learned to serve others. I think about the adventure, work and fun we had so many years ago.

Cook. One experience stands out in my mind. When I was about nine, a local television station featured residents making their favorite recipes on the noon news show. I commented to my mother, "Why do they always have grownups on that show; why don't they ever have kids?" My mother replied, "Well, why don't we call the station and find out?" She called and I was invited to be on the show. My gourmet recipe was peanut butter, honey and banana sandwiches!

Adventurer. We had to assemble a first aid kit to take on a hike. A bandage became useful when my friend Barbara tripped on a rock in the path and fell, injuring her hand.

Pen Pal. We selected names of girls our age, who lived in different countries, to correspond with. I selected Bridget from Ireland and we learned we were not so different even though our lives were lived an ocean apart.

Skating. This brought to mind cold winter weather in Wisconsin where heated ice shacks were a welcome relief. The physical activity and learning balance and strength were important.

Conservation. My dad, a friend and I planted several trees on our property. Several years ago, I was thrilled to see two mammoth trees still standing!

Campcraft. We spent a night at the Wisconsin Dells and had to plan, pack equipment and food, set up, and clean up camp. The fellowship of the girls was as warm as the fire and welcome when darkness fell and there were strange sounds in the night!

Outdoor Cook. We learned how to build a fire safely so we could make s'mores and cook gourmet items, like hot dogs and beans.

Games. The emphasis was on creativity and sportsmanship. Favorite games included jumping rope and playing jacks.

Cyclist. Requirements included keeping a bicycle in good condition, and safety. This was good as my main mode of transportation as a girl was my bicycle.

Personal Health. One requirement was to have a health examination, record what the doctor advised, and carry it out. We also made exhibits about nutrition and good health.

Child Care. As a teenager, my favorite activity and source of income was babysitting. At age 13, a baby brother was added to our family, which further added to my experience.

Homemaker. We made personal budgets, household cleaning duties, cooking, and clean up.

Hospitality. We learned how to be a hostess, get along and converse with people, and table courtesies.

Good Grooming. I learned the correlation between eating healthy food and the condition of my body; and how good grooming is affected by the care of one's possessions, like clothing and shoes.

Besides earning badges, another favorite activity was selling Girl Scout cookies. I was competitive and selling the most cookies was my goal. Back then it was safe to go door to door to sell cookies. One year I sold over 300 dozen boxes and was sure I was in first place. Imagine my dismay when my best friend, Sarah, had her father, who was the president of a company, take orders from all his employees. The lesson learned was that life is not always fair.

My oldest daughter told me when she was a girl, she was amazed at my sash of badges and the story of how I had earned them. Wanting to give back, I was a Brownie Scout leader for her. She remembers going to an apple orchard and singing songs at a nursing home. Once we dyed Easter eggs and I had the opportunity to tell the Resurrection story to these impressionable children. But, the truth must be told that then I really did not know Jesus as my Savior. Years later, when I did accept Him as my Savior, I realized that He used experiences like these to prepare me!

 Parents today do not let children go door-to-door, knocking on strangers' doors alone.

NORTHWEST SCHOOL

The front building on the left side of the picture is where the Lyceum program was held. The larger building behind it is the girls' dorm.

The smaller white building to the right of the girls' dorm was the boys' dorm. The larger white building to the right of the boys' dorm was the Home Ec. building.

The large building in the front portion of the picture is the Field House, which housed the gym. Remaining buildings housed teachers and other adults.

BOARDING SCHOOL DAYS

B. Margaret Bankers

Peg is a published author of several articles in books relating to her Norwegian family. During her 42 years of married life, she and her husband lived in seven different states: North and South Dakota, Minnesota, Kansas, Oklahoma, Texas, and Nebraska. They had five boys and two girls. Her favorite job was the 16 years as a school secretary. Peg moved to Prairie Creek in 2008.

One of my first memories as a child was that my Tabby had kittens in my trundle bed in my parents' bedroom. We lived in a two-bedroom house on a farm in Kittson County, Minnesota. Our house was not insulated and we had no conveniences. We heated the house and cooked with wood and banked it with flax straw to keep the basement from freezing. Temperatures sometimes reached 45 to 50 degrees below zero in January. We were about 80 miles south of Winnipeg.

My brother, Harold, fourteen years older than I, occupied the other bedroom. When I was about six, he left home to find his fortune elsewhere.

I finished elementary school at age 12. My father was a teacher and he encouraged me to go to high school. There were two choices.

My first choice was to go to the local high school ten miles from home and I would board in town during the week.

My second choice was to attend the University of Minnesota Northwest School of Agriculture near Crookston, about 75 miles south of our home.

My parents and I chose NWSA because it provided me with a much better education than any local school could have at that time. We had about 400 students each year, mostly from within a 100-mile area. Most of our teachers were University of Minnesota graduates and many had advanced degrees so students were offered many opportunities for learning. We had a large beautiful campus with many buildings.

At NWSA, the high school year was completed in six months, October to March. This was accomplished by having students attend classes five and one-half days a week. The shortened school year allowed farm students to be home to help with the farming during planting and harvesting. The last high school class graduated in 1965; and currently the campus houses the University of Minnesota at Crookston.

My parents drove me to NWSA on registration day, bringing only one small footlocker with all my belongings. It was disappointing to find the dormitory full and that I was assigned to a bed in the infirmary. Eight girls lived there for a few days until they moved us to a boarding house in the city to live the first semester. I was homesick and wrote my parents to ask them to come and get me. They came, but I had changed my mind and stayed. I moved into the dorm during Christmas break.

I loved high school and took part in many activities. I enjoyed being part of the Speech Choir and made the debate squad. I lettered in debate in 1941 and still have my gold medal "A" for Aggie, which was equivalent to the "A" athletes earned to wear on letter sweaters. It is engraved on the back with my name and the date.

A large part of students' social experience was in the dining hall, which was not a cafeteria line, but tables set for eight or ten with tablecloths and napkins. Upper class students were assigned to be host and hostess for each table and the meal was served family style. Thanksgiving dinner was memorable. Before Thanksgiving Day, the host assigned for each table was required to attend a demonstration to learn how to carve a turkey. Our education was well rounded! The waitresses lined up, each with a big browned turkey on a tray, carried high, one for each table. Many students were on the campus that day because we had classes the next day and, in my case, home was about 75 miles away.

The dining hall was closed after the noon meal on Sundays and we were given a box lunch to be eaten in our rooms Sunday evenings. On other days, after the evening meal, many of us gathered in the Aggie Inn to socialize and perhaps buy a candy bar for a late evening snack. If there was a boyfriend, he probably walked me home, taking a long route, perhaps even to stop and enjoy the warmth of the greenhouse!

On March 15, 1941, after dinner, my friend and classmate, Howard Brandt and I walked to the entrance of the campus. We had a spring thaw and it was warm and still. The atmosphere felt threatening. I remember feeling that threat at the gate where we were out of the shelter of trees. At 7:30, a fierce storm struck the area. We realized how fierce when on Monday, March 18, 1941, the Crookston *Daily Times* headline was: "**67 FOUND DEAD IN NW STORM.**"

Many cars were on the highways on their way to basketball tournaments in the surrounding towns. They were stalled in their tracks and the temperature dropped dramatically. Many tried to walk. The storm raged at least two more days with many inches of snow and high winds. It was a very sobering experience. Some of our faculty was caught in the storm between Crookston and the campus, but I believe all were found safe the next day. Many of us were at the auditorium for a Lyceum program and barely made it back to our dormitory, the next building south. The campus custodian came with a long rope and led many people to the other side of the campus. Even so, they were lost for quite some time. Fortunately, all who were at the program eventually found their way to their homes. This storm happened on a Friday night when many in the general area were on their way to basketball tournaments. There were no weather or blizzard alerts for the Red River Valley.

I was particularly concerned because my roommate had signed out to go home for the weekend, but I knew that she planned to go to Grand Forks to visit her boyfriend. I did not know that she had made it to her farm home instead. ALL WAS WELL AT SCHOOL AGAIN!

I graduated from high school in 1941 and enrolled at Interstate Business College in Fargo, North Dakota, where I finished a secretarial course.

 Today's accurate advanced weather forecasts are used to postpone dangerous weather situations.

HOUSE CLEANING

Robert Fedde

Pastor Fedde and his wife, Lola, retired as former missionaries of the Evangelical Lutheran Church. They lived in Brazil for 17 years and experienced the frontier life on the western edge of the jungle in Western Parana. They have seven children and moved to Prairie Creek from Centerville, SD in February 2007.

In 1960, the Feddes rented a storefront for their living quarters in the new frontier town of Cianorte. The building was made of vertical boards with laths covering the cracks between the hard redwood planks, cracks that harbored many insects. There was no electricity or running water.

One night after going to sleep, we felt something crawling over us under the covers. We awakened with a start! Tiny black ants were everywhere: in our bed, on the walls, floor, and ceiling.

I grabbed our flashlight and saw our bed was too close to the wall where the ants were going up and down and in and out of the cracks. We pushed our bed to the center of the room and the ants left the bed.

They were after insects that were hiding in the walls. Four or five ants would lay hold of the legs of a cockroach, weighing it down as they began dissecting the critter. Crickets and spiders came out of the cracks fleeing for their lives. The numbers of ants overwhelmed the fleeing insects, pulling them into pieces and dragging them back to the jungle brush where they lived.

We went back to sleep. In the morning, our house was totally cleansed of any insects. At the back at the house, we could see the empty path made by the thousands of ants on their way into the jungle. Our house had never been so clean of insects before.

Pastor Fedde has used this experience in children's sermons. Just as Jesus Christ freely died for our sins on a cross, cleansing us from all our sin and then returning to His heavenly home, even so the black ants freely cleansed our house of all insects and then returned to their home in the jungle so that we could live in peace.

The storefront home of Pastor and Mrs. Fedde and their children

PRE-CELL PHONE INGENUITY

Nell Smith

Nell was a small town doctor's wife and mother of five children. She is currently addicted to oil painting and has won first place at South Dakota Masterworks. Another interest is sewing for charity. She has sewn 3,000 tee shirts and 400 sets of matching blankets and caps for babies. Nell moved to Prairie Creek in September 2009.

My husband and I were avid sports fans and never missed a junior high or high school game. We lived in Primghar, Iowa, for approximately 30 years and Andy was the general practitioner along with one other physician. Andy and I had five children and during the course of their school years, two sons played football and one was the football manager.

Back in the late fifties and early sixties, there was no cell phone or pager capability. The hospital was four blocks north of our house and the football field was approximately eight blocks south of the house. The house was a flat-roofed house with a chimney on top. In order for Andy and me to attend the games, he had to devise a mechanism by which the hospital or the town operator could reach him. He devised a lighting system by placing a long pole on top of the house attached to the chimney. He placed a yellow light bulb on the pole and ran a very long extension cord from the roof down into the garage.

FOLLOW THE PIPER

When the children were young, the babysitter would be at home to answer the phones and as the children got older, the babysitter would actually be a "phone sitter." Everyone in town saved our special place just for us on the top bleachers so that whenever there was an emergency or a call for the doctor, the babysitter at our house would go out to the garage and plug in the cord to turn on the light. We could see the light from the top bleacher and everyone would know when there was a yellow light on, that the doctor would be leaving to go back to the house or the hospital to answer the "page." Someone was always available so that I had a ride home. Andy never missed a game; and when the game was out of town, his partner would be the one on call in Primghar.

Back in the fifties, sixties and seventies, there was actually a telephone operator who would keep track of the doctor's whereabouts. The hospital would leave messages with the operator, who would track down Andy at the area town nursing homes or the area hospitals. It was like a central dispatch system where Andy would call the operator and the operator would send messages on to him as needed.

 When a community cooperates, the community wins.

MY PLAYHOUSE

Caroline Schoon

Caroline Schoon is one of four children raised on an average size South Dakota farm during the late thirties. She received her degrees from the University of SD, taught English at USD for 27 years and retired as Professor Emeritus. Caroline and her husband, Robert, who was a geologist, moved to Sioux Falls upon retirement. He passed away in 2009. Caroline moved to Prairie Creek in 2010.

"Grandma, do you know what I have decided to do? I just got this great idea and I can't wait to get started." I was just six at the time and my grandmother often sat and listened to my plans. She lived in a big, beautiful house surrounded by a tall picket fence and a vine-covered canopy over the front entrance. I lived in a smaller house that was on the other side of the farmyard.

"Gracious, child, your cheeks are all red and you're out of breath. Rest a bit while I get you a glass of nectar." She measured out a big spoonful of cherry flavoring into a glass of cool cistern water, added a generous amount of sugar, and then let me stir it all together. Of course, we had no refrigerator and no ice.

I couldn't wait any longer. "You know those two big trees beside the creek in your backyard—those big ones with the big roots above the ground that you said look like a huge hand with gnarly fingers reaching for the water? Well,

I am going to make a playhouse there right by the creek. I have it all planned out and plan to use those roots as steps leading up into the kitchen and living room. And, nobody can get into my playhouse unless they climb those steps. And, the best part is . . ."

"Here, child, take a big drink of nectar and slow down. A playhouse is a fun thing to have, but you know money is really tight during these hard times and there isn't money for extras. You are just going into first grade and maybe you can come up with something easier."

I knew Grandma was trying to help, but my mind was made up. "I've got it all figured out. I've searched the farm's junk pile and I found some pieces of wood and branches, tin cans, and other good stuff I can use. I've got all summer and maybe my cousin Loretta will help."

Grandma was right, it was a big job for a little girl, but I was determined. First, I found some scraps of wood and branches and carefully laid them on the ground so that I could envision two rooms.

I searched for nails, but all I could find were bent, rusty ones. I had seen my dad straighten out those bent nails, so I tried to do the same with the broken hammer that my grandma gave me. It was a hard and painful task and when I would show my grandma my sore fingers, she would just give me sugar cookies and more nectar. She never suggested that I quit the project. In fact, she even gave me a broom with a broken handle. It was just my size. I swept and swept that hard dry dirt until it was shiny, and thought I was a very good housekeeper, just like my mom.

By early summer, I had found such treasures as broken plates, a cracked cup without an ear, and a chipped vase. At peach canning time, Grandma let me have the crates, which made a kitchen cabinet.

At last I pounded pieces of wood onto little logs to make a table and chairs. This was a real challenge as I could never get the nail to go all the way in, but kept pounding until the nail was flat. I don't know for sure, but I suspect my dad helped me a little when I wasn't around.

My family tried hard to let me build my playhouse my way. My favorite piece in the kitchen was the stove. I found a shiny piece of tin for a stovetop, which, of course, helped dry my mud pies. All of my food was beautifully decorated with pebbles, leaves, branches, and seeds. I entertained friends all summer long and my recipes became more elegant by the day. My grandmother often sat on the swing in the screened-in porch and watched me play in my playhouse. I'm sure she found it very entertaining.

One hot Sunday afternoon was one which I shall never forget. Loretta and her family came for a visit. We each had an older brother and an older sister. The girls thought they were "too big" for us and the boys were such teasers that we stayed away from them.

All at once we saw our sisters racing down the hill toward my playhouse. Loretta and I started to yell, "Don't come in here," and "Don't wreck our stuff," but they kept on running past us toward our big swing hanging from one of the trees.

We thought we had scared them off. We did not know that our brothers promised a piece of candy, which was rare at that time, to the one who was the first to get on the swing. They knew Lucille was the fastest runner and they also knew Lucille hated mice. They found a dead mouse and tied it to the rope of the swing and as Lucille won the race, she grabbed the mouse tied to the rope. She frantically jumped up and down and screamed and screamed. Coming down the hill behind them were two 13-year old boys, who were laughing so hard they could hardly stand.

After calming Lucille down, the girls went off in a huff and the boys went the other way, still laughing.

While all of this was going on, Loretta and I stood gaping at the unfolding scene and when the older kids left, we looked at each other, shrugged, and started to giggle.

Now it was time to get busy, so to the playhouse and up the root steps we went into the kitchen. "We've got baking to do, so let's get busy."

Each summer I rebuilt the playhouse and each year it got easier. I wonder if my dad put the small logs in front of the pile without saying anything to me, making it easier to rebuild each year. Knowing my dad, he would!

Now that I look back at all those wonderful years in my playhouse, I don't remember anyone saying things like "Don't step on a nail or you will get a bad infection" or "Don't play with those dirty things from the junk pile."

We were never vaccinated for anything and were allowed to roam the entire farm. With the little that we had, a child in the '30s had to use her imagination and energy to accomplish dreams that last a lifetime.

 Children today are not often challenged to creatively seek their own entertainment.

THE PEPPERMINT BULL

Virgil Miller

Virgil and his wife, Louise, raised a family of eight children. They loved to travel during slow times and visited all 50 states, eight European countries, Canada and Mexico. They are avid sports fans, enjoying baseball and basketball.

Farming in the West River region involves a lot of work and a lot of luck. The people are honest, hard workers and are always ready to help anyone in need. Like most small towns, we had a café with a big table where the farmers gathered in the mid-morning and about 3:00 in the afternoon. On rainy days, when they couldn't work, there was always a big crowd and the jokes and stories were hilarious. Most every tale was greatly exaggerated. If it was harvest time and one fellow would tell his wheat yield was making 50 bushels to the acre, you could bet someone else would tell of 52, and the next day someone's yield would be 54 and so on. Whoever told first always had the poorest yield.

The same went for the weight of their calves in the fall. I had been farming for a few years and always wanted a few head of livestock. I got the chance to lease a ranch 30 miles north of Presho, in Stanley County, so I jumped at the opportunity. I had 800 ewes, which produced about 1,000

79

lambs a year. We always fattened the lambs and sold them at the Sioux Falls Livestock Company. My lambs were the BEST of quality and always brought top money for the day.

My cows were a different story. The calves always sold way lower than the best. I needed to upgrade my herd, so I decided to buy the best bull I could find. There was a bull show at an auction in Presho; I think it was either in March or April. I went to the show and the Grand Champion was really SOMETHING; long and lean and well-muscled. I HAD TO HAVE HIM. That night at the auction I bought him, but paid more than I wanted to pay. I took him home and put him in the corral. I didn't want him with the cows until June 1st so we would get spring calves. I fed him my best hay and a little grain each day. Too much grain would make him fat and lazy. June 1st came and I chased him out in the pasture so he could start mating with my cows. OH, WHAT AN ANIMAL HE WAS!! I went back to the barn to finish up a little work and then went to the house for lunch.

When I came outside after lunch, there was my prize bull back in the corrals eating hay. I WAS DEVASTATED! So, I went to town to visit the veterinarian to see if he could figure out what to do. He told me he had just gotten some experimental pills that were supposed to put a little life into a bull. I bought the WHOLE big bottle and headed for the ranch. I quickly got the bull in the cattle chute, got about five feet of garden hose and put it down his throat. I dropped two little blue pills in it so they would go directly into his stomach.

I noticed when I was putting the pills away that the bull wanted to get out of the chute. I opened the head gate and he jumped out, pawing the ground with his head held high, sniffing the air. All at once, his tail went high into the air, he let out a couple of snorts and headed toward the cows in the pasture on a dead run. For the next five years, my calves always topped the mark. OH, WHAT A BULL!

Several people have asked me for the name of those pills, but all I know is that they were experimental and they are all gone now. BUT, I can tell you that they had a peppermint taste.

That's my story and I'm sticking to it!

IT TAKES A COMMUNITY

Jim Leffler

Being born in 1945 puts Jim on the leading edge of the baby boomer generation. He grew up in Illinois, and lived in Oklahoma, New York, Minnesota, Arizona, and South Dakota. Jim served in the Air Force working with flight simulators and retired from IBM in 1997. At 55, Jim and his wife, Jan, retired to Clarksdale, AZ. They joined the Prairie Creek Community in October 2006.

My story is told through the eyes of a youth. It takes place in the '50s, describing the history and impact a community has on an individual. A community provides life skills and nurtures one toward adulthood. West Liberty, Illinois, sits a half-mile off the main highway, 15 blocks square, 120 residents, and the IC railroad running through the center. It is located 200 miles south of Chicago and 100 miles east of St. Louis.

In 1947, I arrived in West Liberty at the ripe old age of two and three-fourths. Now, at that age, I remember little except dinners at Grandma's. Oh, but what a town! It was by far the most important place on the earth. A small farming community with mixed residency of retirees, commuters, and business personnel, I dare say there are NO words to describe the fondness I have for my little community. My memories are of caring neighbors, church, school, and annual events.

Our property consisted of four lots; two for home and garden and two fenced for livestock, with a barn and chicken coop. School was a block away; church two blocks away; and the business district with a post office, just three blocks away. As an adventurous child, I was able to explore all corners of my town. On our farm, we kept chickens for eggs and fryers, pigs for food and litters for market, and Bessie the cow for milk and calves; remember, no calves, no milk. In the hayloft, we had cats with kittens and hiding places for kids.

One year our sow gave birth to a litter of thirteen piglets, all were cute as a button. Mom, ever caring Mom, came through like a trooper. She scooped up the runt, made a home out of a box, and we kept Pinky behind the potbellied stove in the kitchen and hand fed her. Mom created a potion, "DEEPLY HELD SECRET FAMILY RECIPE," which was milk in a baby bottle with a precise proportion of love, and it worked. Before long, Pinky grew up and had to be returned to the barnyard. One small problem, Pinky now believed she was human. Many a day Pinky would crawl under the fence and came squealing at the back door for attention. We'd feed Pinky out of a dish and add a scratch or three behind the ear. Pinky would then crawl back under the fence, returning to the barnyard. One day Pinky disappeared and how I cried; unbeknownst to me, it was time for Pinky to return our love.

School was just a block away. I can still see dozens of children laughing and playing. Even before I attended school, I would hear the children during recess and join them. When recess was over, I returned home and could hardly wait for the next one. At six, I entered first grade and never, except maybe when in trouble, did I miss a recess.

Oh, how I loved my first and second grade teacher. She was like a grandmother to all students. Grace kept immaculate flower gardens, and what I remember most is the majestic clump of original prairie grass standing five feet tall and waving gracefully in the breeze. The school only had three classrooms, grades 1-2, 3-5, and 6-8 in their respective room.

Many happy times were spent at the Methodist church. There was much excitement in '55 because our church was expanding by building a basement. The excitement arose because we had to raise the church for excavation. My job was to crawl under the church, place the screw jack, and turn the screw when the maestro directed me. Every screw jack required an attendant because the church had to be raised evenly.

Also within the church was a Ladies' Aid group that quilted and did fundraisers. My favorite was Chowder Day. The menu consisted of chowder, Sloppy Joes, homemade ice cream, pies, and cakes served in the evening to hundreds. The day started early in the morning and went way into the evening. Families worked and shared earth's bounty from farm and garden to create a creamy stew like chowder. The chowder recipe is another "VERY DEEPLY HELD SECRET." You need large pots, ladles for stirring, fire, meat and vegetables, and then sprinkle in just the right amount of love from neighbors and community. I beg of you, please don't tell the elders that I let the cat out of the bag.

About the people of my community, leading the list is my parents, a sister five years older, a brother four years younger, and my grandma, who lived on the other side of the tracks. Whoops! I shouldn't use the track thing because everyone in my community is special, no worse, no better. On our block was my teacher, Grace, and her postmaster husband; a contractor with a block factory; a retired farmer; a retired railroader, who raised strawberries; and a very cute retired couple. The husband drove with the wife, who sat in the middle front seat just like teenagers. Seatbelts had not been invented yet. Another retired railroader, who kept all of his money in his billfold tucked away in the top pocket of his bib overalls, lived about a block away. He would show his money to us kids. I don't know how much money he had, but it must have been at least a million! There were hundreds and fifties galore.

There was a special lady, who I only remember as being a recluse. Her lot, house and all, were completely fenced, blinds pulled; and I never saw a light on. I called her the Goat Lady because she kept goats in the yard, presumably for milk, cheese, and meat. She kept a neat garden, but I rarely saw her gardening.

My friends and I would go rabbit hunting, shooting our limit almost every time, rabbits being plentiful. Unable to use all the rabbits, I decided to share them with the Goat Lady. Even when I called to her, she would not come out to receive them. Then I threw the rabbits over the fence thinking she would respond, but no such luck. I would wait and wait; still no response. Now, not able to retrieve the rabbits, I just left, returning a short time later, and to my amazement, the rabbits were gone. Even without a thank you, I shared my bounty for many a season. To this day I know I was helping a friend in need and the rabbits never went to waste.

As a youngster, I realized even in a small community, there were jobs to be performed. No matter how small the job, someone had to perform them. My jobs were never listed with the city council, as none existed; nor was I appointed a commissioner. But, I did take it upon myself to do the job. Mr. Newman, father of a classmate, would get out the steel-wheeled tractor and drag the gravel streets, knocking down the crowns and filling the potholes. Two or three Saturdays a year the drag would come out, the word would spread, and every available child in town would jump on the drag for a five-mile ride. The riders created weight, which made the drag bite into the crown and push gravel forward, filling in the potholes. You see, if you don't explain to children that this is work, they'll be having fun.

Now on to a really fun job; this happened when we had wind storms and how it did blow, tornadoes and all. Limbs blew off, trees blew down, and buildings were damaged. Men from town and farm showed up with saws, axes, and tractors. Boy, did my eyes light up and my heart go a-flitter when the tractors arrived. By now I was twelve or so and the farmers would let me drive their tractors. I dare say there's not a more important job than driving the tractor and pulling brush into a pile on an empty lot. After the cleanup, the community would gather to have a wiener roast with s'mores in celebration that no one was injured and for a job well done.

This wonderful town had a junk yard, a wonderful and adventurous place. One could find things for play, building, bottles to break, and treasures. Red rubber inner tubes were sought for slingshots or rubber band guns, which made tubes as valuable as gold. Black, or synthetic rubber, was now being produced, but wasn't nearly as elastic. Kids would trade precious toys for red rubber strips; I should know, I traded a metal filling station for a slingshot.

I couldn't break every bottle because I knew a lady who collected bottles. She was another special lady I named the "Bottle Lady." In my diggings I would find a unique bottle, take it, knock on her door, and when she answered, I would ask if she had this one in her collection. I distinctly remember her answer, "Oh, why no." She'd ask where I found the bottle, thank me, and happily say she would add it to her collection. I saw her collection many times and she always pointed out which bottles I had brought her; she was surely special.

Later, the junkyard played an important part in my life by providing me with a real job. I borrowed Dad's Ford N tractor and the neighbor's two-wheeled cart. Of course, I drove. This is how I learned to drive, back up, and even to do a little work. You see, I would haul junk or move anything for a little money. But money was not my real goal because just being able to drive anything, at fourteen, was pay enough.

In '54, there was a severe drought and many a well went dry. The drought was so bad, the discussion around town was whether the community needed a rainmaker. There were traveling rainmakers showing up and offering their services. Water-witchers were also in high demand; some people used them, but my dad just picked out a good spot and started digging. A well was six feet across and twenty feet deep or until water was reached. The dirt from the well had to be shoveled into buckets, hoisted to the surface, and hauled away. After finding water, the well was lined with brick. The top eight feet was mortared to stop surface water from entering. Times being tough, one's hope was to get the bricks free. As luck would have it, dad knew the owner of a fallen brick house. We picked bricks and hauled them home. The old mortar had to be removed from the bricks, so I went to work with hammer and chisel. I tried the Tom Sawyer trick, but no takers. You see, the kids of the '50s, being of great intelligence, had already learned that story. Our well came in, others were not so lucky; some struck water at the same time their neighbors went dry. The latter left many hard feelings if you had hit "my" vein of water.

While growing up, I didn't realize the community was actually dying before my very eyes, even though everyone was working hard to keep it alive. No one discussed the dwindling of either business or the railroad. Then the inevitable happened; late one evening in the fall of '58, the general store burned down. After dark, while everyone watched the flames turn to ash, the question on everyone's mind was, "Will the owner rebuild?" The answer came back, "NO." Today, I realize this was the straw that broke the camel's back; West Liberty, as I knew it, had come to an end. Everyone had family ties to the once thriving community and we expected the town to last forever.

Today, only the memories remain, but how great they are. My dad also grew up there during the Depression and I'm so blessed to have received the opportunity to walk in his footsteps. I know many elders tell me about the '30s, but according to my parents, it was no bed of roses in the '50s either. I now know how big an impact West Liberty had on my life.

 Keep your memories alive by touching someone else's life as they touched yours.

ESCAPE FROM THE CITY

Lynn Assimacopoulos

In midsky the sun rests brilliantly.
The air grasps echoes
Of a lone dog's bark.
Soft feathered shining swans
Slide upon the clear water
In the quiet of the park.

Pure field-flavored breezes
Flow through open windows
Across a napping child,
Then turn to fill the kitchen
Where on the old oak table
Fresh garden vegetables are piled.
A lone car glides slowly
In front of a dusty gravel cloud
As the wind rustles in the corn.
At dusk, rainbows of flowers
Close their soft shaped petals
Waiting patiently for a new morn.

Unlocked painted wood doors
Welcome stranded strangers
With warm bread and a coffee filled cup.
Then "stranger" turned into "friend"...
Leaves with a handshake, a smile and a wave—
Time for escape from the city is up.

THE CAR IN THE CORNFIELD

Lynn Assimacopoulos

I remember the car in the cornfield,
Dented fenders and wheels all flat,
We ran to sit in it every day,
Me with my doll and he with his hat.
Across whole countries and nations we "rode,"
Imaginary travels so free,
Exploring each and every town,
And then stopping for occasional "tea."
Oh, what a wonderful car it was,
It's magic known only to us two,
And he who was almost six years old,
Said, "You know I do love you."
"And when we grow up" promised he,
"We will marry and then celebrate
With a long and wonderful ride
Visiting each and every state.
I smiled and gave him a tiny kiss,
His promise was stated and sealed.
How lucky was I who was only five
To have him and that car in the cornfield.

Arlette (Peterson) Villaume at 13 years of age in 1942.

ALL THINGS WORK TOGETHER FOR GOOD

Arlette Villaume

Arlette moved to Prairie Creek in May 2009 from Corpus Christi, TX. She is a graduate of Augustana College and earned a MSW from the University of Chicago. She worked many years as therapist, educator and Mental Health administrator. Arlette's family includes four children, nine grandchildren and three great-grandchildren.

Life on the farm was never easy, but during the '30s, called the "dust-bowl" years in the Midwest, farm life challenged the strength and faith of everyone. Dried or diseased crops meant little income during a national depression. Dried out pastures meant young children herded cattle wherever morsels might be found, such as along the roadsides and fence lines.

Our father tied a rope from the house to the barn to insure our safety when the dust storms were as blinding as the worst snowstorms. Some days, dust caused such darkness that kerosene lamps were needed in school; and the country school teacher held children there until parents came to take them home safely.

During those years when there was no money to pay "hired men" to help with farm work, most children needed to learn early to do whatever they could, including field work using horses or tractor, milking cows or whatever they were able. Little did we know that the rough life of the "dirty thirties" actually became a blessing as it prepared us to assume adult roles when our father, at age 40, suddenly became a total invalid in 1938. My brother and I, at ages 15 and 12, had to assume responsibility for all the farm work; and my sister and younger brother, at ages 9 and 4, had to help mother with chores, including housekeeping and care of our father. Sometimes that meant turning a page when he could read, scratch a nose that itched or chase an irritating fly; something even a 4-year-old could do.

Even if there had been money to pay for help, World War II had drained the area of possible manpower. During the school year, cows were milked before and after school, and all other work was done on weekends. In the spring, we were excused from school for several weeks to get crops seeded. Fortunately, passing exams was all the teachers required of us.

My father's illness was never diagnosed except to recognize that all the nerves in his body were inflamed, causing extreme pain. Medical journals reported no other case like it. During the first six months, there were only three places on his body that mother could touch to move him. Even the footsteps of an active 4-year-old crossing the floor of an old house caused excruciating pain. The six-month prognosis seemed realistic because by then he could not even close his eyes and we could not tell if he was asleep. One Easter Eve our faithful country doctor stated he did not expect dad would live until morning.

But, with God-given determination and a heart that would not stop, he lived another 5½ years. Despite all our efforts to improve mobility, he was never again able to use his hands or feet.

Many years later, my mother said, "I am so sorry that your childhood was taken from you because of Dad's illness." That Mother's Day, in addition to thanking her for being such a wonderful and special mother, I listed all the unusual and unexpected blessings and gifts we received from our father, which far exceeded any inconvenience and suffering we experienced. A special gift was that his keen mind was spared so he was able to give us all the guidance and knowledge we needed in order to plan, organize and face any challenge that would arise. He taught us not to fear failure, but to look for better solutions to a problem. When machinery would break down, he taught us problem-solving techniques that we have continued to use all our lives. We learned early the joy of work and of accomplishing a task. We always felt needed. The value of teamwork to get everything done was reinforced every day. All of these gifts resulted in our accepting positions and responsibilities that later in life we otherwise would have been afraid to tackle. How blessed we have been!

There was always love and respect for each other in our family, but like most Norwegians in those days, there was no public display of affection. I do not remember our parents hugging or kissing in our presence. However, one day after we had helped strengthen Dad's arms so he could lift them higher than six inches, I happened to enter the room where dad was reclining in his wheelchair while mother leaned over to comb his hair. For the first time he was able to lift his arms and embrace her for a few seconds. The sheer joy in their laughter and the passionate love in their gaze was the most beautiful expression of love that I have ever witnessed. I did not wait to see if they "sealed it with a kiss" because I felt I had already invaded "holy ground."

The greatest blessing and gift was the faith that mother and dad lived and passed on to us. They never complained or questioned "Why?" They accepted each day as it came and taught us to trust that God would always be with us and give us what we need.

Our dad's greatest gift was to no longer fear death because he also taught us how to die. As we sat beside his bedside, he told us how much he loved us and how proud he was of us. He punctuated so much of his life with singing, whether he was milking cows, working in the field, driving the car or enjoying gathered family; so it was not at all strange that he reverted to softly humming or singing an old Norwegian hymn, **"Flee as a bird to the mountain you who are weary of sin. Flee to the fast flowing fountain where you may wash and be clean."** It ends with the words that Jesus will come and **"He to his bosom will bear thee."** I was taking his fading pulse rate when Dad smiled and confidently announced, **"Now, I'm going HOME!"**

Mother's only statement after I announced that Dad's heart had stopped was "Thank God, he doesn't have to suffer any more." I went into the next room to tell Grandma that her son had died. With tears welling in her eyes, she said, "I had twelve children, now only six are left." Then I went to the porch steps where our younger brother was sitting with his arm around the dog, Bing. With as much a statement as a question he said, "Dad died." With my arm around him, I shared what had just happened and told him how much Dad loved him and how proud he was of him.

 Children of the Depression era learned family values along with physical labor at an early age.

THE HOLLYHOCKS

Lynn Assimacopoulos

With royal hue the colors shown as if in a special kingdom,
Amidst the morning dew their open petals could be seen from afar.
The hands that touched and twisted the vines each day
Spoke softly saying, "I will take care of you."

The blossoms returned the warmth with whispered multicolored thank-yous.
No other hand could rule their ground.
No other eyes would gaze on them so.
Then one day the hands touched them no more.

The smiles and whispers came no more.
And the world of hues and colors shown no more.
For several risings of the sun and kingdom lives in darkness.
Then rebirth appeared the day the master gardener was buried beneath the ground.

The hues of remembrance once more shown.
And the mystery of this shall be known only to
The hands that twisted and touched
And whispered to the honoring blooms.
Good-bye, good-bye, good-bye, kind and wise old man of the garden.

Valentine's Day 2008:

"Tom was wearing the Queen's crown,
The Royal robe, and
sat next to the King."

ROYALTY AT THE LODGE

Mary Anderson

Mary is the Activity Director at Prairie Creek and one of her fun activities is to plan the Valentine coronation of King and Queen. The royalty is chosen by popular vote and Mary buys the presents, gets the crown and robes out of storage and plans the coffee party.

The votes had been counted and I knew Ruth Ludgate had been elected Queen and Keith Jensen was the King. Everything was ready including the royal chairs, which were placed in front of the fireplace. I was the only one who knew the results of the vote.

I noticed that Tom Ludgate and Keith walked into the Library together and breathed a sigh of relief at the sight of the new King. However, Tom's wife, the newly elected Queen, was nowhere in sight, so I decided to wait a bit for her arrival. Ruth was a very deserving Queen with her friendly demeanor and long record of volunteering at Prairie Creek, her church, and the hospital.

Finally, I knew I could wait no longer. I asked the new King to come forward and placed the crown and robe on him as I quietly asked if he knew where Ruth was. Keith replied, "Tom told me that she was delivering some treats to their son." Keith said that when he was sitting with Tom

FOLLOW THE PIPER

he asked, "Could you try to find your wife because I am certain she is the missing Queen."

Tom's sight is impaired due to macular degeneration. Because he didn't want to be too obvious, he bent over as far as he could and tried to use his cell phone without success. But, he kept trying and hadn't noticed that Keith was on the throne.

Tom came up for air and heard the new King call him to the royal throne. Surprised to find the King already crowned, Tom approached the King and me. "Any luck?" inquired the King.

Tom replied, "I can't find her anywhere," then added, "Who is the missing Queen?"

The King asked, "Tom, would you sit in for the Queen on a temporary basis because I don't want Ruth to totally lose out as the new Queen."

Tom agreed and after a short announcement to the residents, Tom was wearing the Queen's crown, the royal robe and sat next to the King.

By this time, the good citizens of Prairie Creek were enjoying the commotion and a lot of laughing ensued, along with some comments that weren't so complimentary, but were meant in good fun.

When things settled down, the party continued. One of the residents entered the Library about that time, analyzed the situation and upon sitting down, tersely muttered, "This time I think we crossed the line and I don't approve. We have gone too far here at Prairie Creek and I don't like it!"

Tom and Keith spend many hours together getting each other straightened out or more confused. Often, they attract other residents and that's when the fun really gets going. The two guys agree that it's a great hideout from their wives as they babysit each other late into the evening.

The elected Valentine King and Queen:
Keith Jensen and Ruth Ludgate

THE GOLDEN HARVEST

Mary George

Mary and her husband, Cyril, moved to Prairie Creek in 2008. They enjoyed farming with their four children. Mary has always enjoyed volunteering. At Prairie Creek, Mary tends flower and vegetable gardens, sews, quilts and paints in her spare time. Cyril makes caps for infants and donates them to a local hospital.

Dad came in for dinner and put a handful of oat stalks on the kitchen table. Yesterday, he had pulled the binder out of the shed and checked it over carefully, including the canvas that moves the oat straws from the cutting bar to the knotter. The knotter gathers the stalks together into a bundle and ties them with twine. The family would gather about six bundles in a shock so the oats would continue to dry before the threshing began. We knew there was an adventure ahead and we welcomed the news of the threshing season.

It was the middle of July and we noticed the oat heads were rapidly turning from their beautiful green to gold. The summer sun had pretty much finished the maturing process and now we were in for some hard work. The binder would circle the oats field until all the oats had been put into bundles and six or seven bundles would be put together in shocks to let the oats dry. We knew the weather would be hot every day, but we also knew what was needed to bring the harvest home. We children faced the next week with anticipation and joy in our hearts. The hot sun would require a lot of work, but it also meant a lot of fun.

The harvest would be extra work beyond the regular chores that needed to be done twice a day: milking the cows, the chicken chores and tending the animals. Unless we had finished pulling the cockleburs and cutting sunflowers, it also meant walking the cornfields to finish that summer job.

In addition to Mom's usual work, she was already planning the two big dinners that she would provide for the threshing crew. She had decided roast beef, potatoes mashed with cream, gravy and several vegetables would need to be prepared the first day for the threshing crew. Morning lunch would be hauled out to the threshing rig and an afternoon lunch would also be expected.

We had been alerted to watch for at least five big roosters that would provide the second dinner. In the early spring my dad had ordered a straight run of baby chicks, which meant that we could expect about 50 roosters for spring frying and about 50 pullets that would be added to the chicken house for eggs. Mom was the chicken "boss" and took pride in raising the chickens.

The shocks had been left undisturbed for several weeks when Dad announced that the neighbors who were in the threshing ring had met and decided to start threshing the next Monday. Our farm headed the list. It would take about two weeks to finish at the five farms. Once threshing was complete at our place, the rig would be moved to the next neighbor. My dad and brother would help at the neighbors; and the rest of us knew that we were expected to pick up the slack around the farm, which included extra cow milking and feeding the livestock. Of course, there would be weeds for us to chop and other things the men and boys would usually do.

Mom made a list of things that needed to be done. She didn't need the list, but it was a way of alerting the rest of us about all that needed to be done. A table for washing would be set up outside so the men could wash their dirty hands and sweaty faces before dinner. Extra supplies needed to be purchased ahead of time as there wouldn't be time to run into town in the midst of food preparation. Leaves for the table had to be located so the table would seat sixteen; maybe more would be at the kitchen table. The house had to be put in order. It would be good to have the washing out of the way so Monday and Tuesday could be used for the threshers.

Our farm didn't have electricity or running water, which made Mom's job harder, but she had been through it all before. Dad had put a barrel beside the windmill with a pipe running through it so the cold water would provide a cool place to store things. We used a similar setup to keep our cream cool so it wouldn't sour before the creamery picked it up three times a week.

Monday morning came early for all of us. By the time we came in for breakfast, mom had bread and rolls baking in the cook stove. She was squeezing lemons for pie and the crusts were cooling on the counter. Dad had been to town and brought back sweet rolls for morning coffee, a block of ice and a big roast beef.

Mom knew she had to get the baking done so the roast beef could go into the cook stove oven. The cook stove was heated with cobs or wood and had to be watched carefully to keep it at the best temperature for cooking and baking. The reservoir at the opposite end needed to be filled with water so we would have warm water for washing dishes. The kitchen windows brought in some fresh air to help cool the kitchen, but it was still a hot place all day.

We heard the steel-rimmed tractor coming slowly into our driveway, pulling the threshing machine to the place my dad said he wanted the threshing done. Both the oats and the straw were valuable. The straw stack had to be carefully placed so in the winter months it could be used as bedding for the livestock.

All of us, except Mom, were outside at once to watch the parade. Soon the neighbors arrived with their hayracks pulled by a team of beautiful horses. In addition to the usual harness, each horse had a nose basket and fly nets to keep the flies from biting them since this could lead to runaways and wrecked racks. The flies would crawl into the horses' sensitive noses and bite them. The nose baskets also kept the horses from nibbling on the oats and straying from their job of pulling the racks.

The men trained the horses to obey their voice commands. When the farmer had picked up the bundles at one shock, a word or two was all that was needed to get the horses to move down the row.

My job those two days consisted of helping mom pack the lunches to go to the field. Hot coffee, cold water, sweet rolls and sandwiches were moved to the threshing rig. After dinner, the pile of dishes was huge; they needed to be washed, dried and put away. The usual dirty dishes were also there, including the separator, which had been used to separate the fresh cow's milk from the cream.

These days created wonderful memories of a busy, but wonderful harvest season. Love and hard work brought us all together as a family and a community.

After threshing was complete, the owner of the threshing rig hosted a party for everybody. It was time to relax and enjoy the company of one another. There was beer for the men and pop for the kids, along with homemade treats for everybody.

 The harvest is gathered by the community with grateful hearts.

BLACK, WHITE OR GRAY

Thomas Vanden Bosch

Wanting more than a high school education, Tom enrolled in high school at age 24. After graduating college and seminary, he served as a parish pastor and was a chaplain at mental and veteran hospitals. Tom and his wife moved into Prairie Creek in 2008. They have three children.

My story begins as a boy in a tight-knit prairie farm community. We had things worked out in terms of right and wrong. Everything was black or white and there were no gray areas to worry about, and, looking back, I wasn't even aware of gray areas. Let me give you an example.

In our Dutch community, church membership and attendance were givens. On Sunday, one did not mow a lawn, wash a car, or go shopping. Children were cautioned to play on the back porch, not the front one. Arrangements were worked out not only for Sundays, but in all areas such as theology, moral behavior, and work ethics. Life was very tight, but worked well.

Neighboring communities of Danish, Norwegian, German, and Italians operated much the same, although the basic beliefs would vary from one community to another. One community allowed liquor to be sold and consumed, others went shopping on Sunday, and some encouraged membership in lodges. But, as a Dutch boy, I was well aware of what was expected of me.

In church, I was taught the right answers to the questions of faith, life, and behavior, and I memorized the answers to some of the tougher concepts. I don't, however, remember being asked what I believed or thought or felt. It was all black or white; no gray areas.

None of this bothered me much as I earned my GED and graduated from college and seminary. It was when I became a father that my real education began.

My oldest son at age five was troubled by something he could not explain to me and I could not figure out what to do for him. We tried doctors, medicines, and therapies; even a chiropractor thinking it was a nerve problem. All I really understood was that I loved him and I prayed for help and guidance.

When my son became a teenager, he was better able to explain his feelings. I tried to understand what he was saying and I assured him that I loved him. But, what he was telling me didn't square with my black or white world as I had been taught.

My son in sincere agony explained the best he could how he was feeling and shared that it was so distressful that he had been thinking suicide would be best for everybody. His message was consistent and simple: his attraction was not for girls, it was for boys. He knew it was wrong and once he had taken the "H" encyclopedia and went to a private spot to read about homosexuality.

I found myself, an ordained minister and a loving father, not knowing what to do. I explained to him that he was very young and at the end of puberty his outlook would probably change and life would be good.

Knowing that I might have to face this issue in the future, I began a very thorough search of the topic in the Bible and through position papers and periodicals.

The one thing I was always sure of was my unconditional love for my son. However, the word "reprobate" from my Bible burned in my heart. Was my son headed for hell and, if so, was there anything I could do about it? Should I try to talk him out of it? Maybe counseling? Maybe medical intervention?

My son, now a young man, remained celibate, and I continued to dialog as time wore on. He transferred his desire for his own children by becoming "Super Uncle." He shared that he wanted to be in a committed relationship.

The reprobate issue was not solved in my mind. Was it possible that I might lose my son to the fire of damnation by accepting his gay lifestyle? I searched my soul. Maybe there was a gray area, maybe it wasn't a black or white issue. Perhaps that could be an answer.

My son announced that he had accepted a new position in Washington, DC. The news came that he had a partner. A change of address made what he was sharing with me final: He was in a committed relationship.

I knew, of course, that it was his decision and he would be held accountable, but I was concerned about my own involvement. Closest to my heart was the responsibility that remained: He was my son and I would continue my unconditional love for him as I searched for direction as to how to solve this situation.

Arrangements were made for my wife and me to visit him, his partner, his church, and his friends in Washington, DC. The answer to my long-held question came while we attended his church and met his friends: men, women, children, gay, straight, old, young. And, red and yellow, black and white, just as I had sung as a young boy in my Dutch church. They are all precious in HIS sight.

God had made them all! Indeed, they were all precious. And, it was a black and white issue: **ALL ARE PRECIOUS IN HIS SIGHT!**

ONLY BUT NOT LONELY CHILD

Peryl Beckman

It was somewhat unusual for Peryl to be an only child as most of the neighbor children had five or six brothers and sisters. But Peryl's parents had lots of company and relatives to visit. On the farm, Peryl had animal pets, including baby mice. She and her husband had five children. Peryl moved into Prairie Creek in 2007.

My parents eloped and homesteaded in Montana. After several tries, including a fire that wiped them out, they returned to South Dakota where I grew up. My parents and I survived the flu epidemic of 1918.

Country school was two miles away and a neighbor boy and I walked together. I was afraid of cows and walked out of sight until I got past the pasture. Dad would take us by horse and buggy or the bobsled on nasty days.

The neighbor boy and I usually got along pretty well. Math was hard for him so I did his work and he paid me in coins until Mother found out. There went my first paying job. Some days I chased him home with a stick when he teased me.

When I was eleven, I became ill at school and the teacher said I should walk home. When I got home, my parents weren't there so I put myself to bed. When they got home, I had a high fever and was out of my head. Mother was scared because a fortune teller once told her she would lose a child. A doctor was called, who lived eleven miles away. He said I had pneumonia.

For weeks, my Mother and the neighbor ladies kept cold towels on my head and chest night and day. I had weird visions. Once I saw my uncle bring a pie and I kept saying he was fooling me, I knew it was a jack o' lantern. Another time I was reading to some children and I kept telling them to get away because I couldn't breathe, but they kept coming closer.

My uncle suggested that we should try his Indian Oil that he brought back from Oklahoma. It was smeared on my chest, back and neck. Three days later the fever broke. The doctor was paid for all his visits with a calf. I missed three months of school.

The doctor said I could have anything I wanted so I asked for watermelon. Watermelon was out of season and when the pool hall owners heard of my request, they sent a case of orange soda. We never had pop so that was a big treat.

I always felt lucky to recover from pneumonia, but I had some unlucky scrapes also. I have fallen off many horses, out of trees, over rocks and while roller-skating. I've had a broken leg, a broken arm, gallstones, kidney stones, three surgeries and five children. Once I hurt my leg and my mom bandaged it with salt pork. When I went out to play, it attracted some dogs and I had to fight them off.

My earliest sex education was received from my cousin's friend, who knew all about babies. We took off all our clothes just as my aunt came in. By the way, my cousin was a boy.

We had house dances. Our neighbor had a small band and we had a small piano. I usually danced every dance and even ate lunches with the boys. I have to admit of having a few crushes.

My father owned a threshing machine so my mother and I would follow the machine around the neighborhood

FOLLOW THE PIPER

and help the other women with the food preparation. I loved this time of year. As I got older I enjoyed getting to know the boys who helped out.

I married my husband and both of us had a few education credits so we could teach school. As time went on, we put a lot of our time, money and energy into earning more credits and better jobs. Education was our life's work.

At age 50, I earned my BA. We moved thirteen times, not counting the time I followed my husband while he was in the service.

I took care of Mother, who was nearly blind for the last 15 years of her life.

At 92, I'm still here. Thank you, God.

 Penicillin was first used to treat pneumonia in 1946. Until then, pneumonia was often fatal.

GRASSHOPPERS

Sylvia Fuoss

Sylvia and her husband, Floyd, farmed and ranched in West River, South Dakota where they raised five children. At age 50, Sylvia entered the University of Minnesota, earning her Doctorate in Housing Design while working for the Minnesota Extension Service. After retiring in April 2006, Sylvia and Floyd moved to Prairie Creek.

I grew up with grasshoppers. They colored my childhood; it seemed they were the only living green around.

I was born in a tiny one-story nursing home in Presho, where our bachelor doctor had his office. My father came the eight miles of gumbo and five miles of gravel roads in our 1928 Chevrolet car to bring the two of us home. He often recalled the shock he felt as, leaving town on US Highway 16, the car began to swerve uncertainly. The road was swarming alive with some kind of large insects new to his experience. "Sylvia and the grasshoppers arrived the same year the banks went broke," he often remarked. That was June of 1931, and he told the story as a joke to soften the reality of what the grasshopper infestation meant.

The corn he had planted early was up and lush when he left for Presho. We arrived home to find the corn completely gone, with only the mounds of the lister rows to mark where it had stood. The grasshoppers were alien to our farm before that, but they had arrived in such volume that they made clouds that shaded the sun. The hoppers coated nearly everything, eating whatever they could. They crowded on the sunrise side of buildings and fence posts and moved to the shady side as the heat rose. When they ate the paint off the house, we hoped the lead in the paint might kill a few. As we forked hay to the livestock, the precious bundles would be alive with those chewing insects. But Mother's turkeys would eat them, and that was no small matter, since the income provided our winter's bounty.

Mostly, we just gave up competing with the hoppers for edibles, but there were a few plants they would not eat. Every spring, my sisters and I were sent to the road ditches to harvest young sprigs of lamb's quarter that was served like spinach. Hoppers only ate sparingly of Swiss chard, which I considered inedible. They must not have had any common sense.

Shortly before my birth, my Grandmama had come to visit and suffered a stroke. She could not speak, or move on her own and remained completely dependent on my mother's care. We lived quietly, so we would not disturb her. The family admonished me: "Don't cry, because if you cry, Grandmama will cry." I looked into the bedroom to see the sun shining through her wispy white hair, and I was quiet. To lift our spirits, my sisters would play the piano, our parents would dance to the beat and Grandmama would laugh. I was told I would hop up and down in my crib to the music and hum the melody. Those tough times came to an end when Grandmama passed away from another stroke about the time of my third birthday.

One spring I asked my father what it would be like on my birthday. He replied that it would be so hot and dry that I would be able to go outside and put my feet into the cracks in the ground. On June 8th, I checked that out by fitting my foot deep into a crack. To break our sorrow, he brought home ice from town and we had homemade ice cream with my birthday cake. The next month, we splurged with ice cream again, and one rocket to celebrate Independence Day. Sometimes it took some discipline to find a happy occasion.

The weather didn't give us much to enjoy. It was hot and dry in summer; and cold and stormy in winter, with a constant wind. The dust bowl arrived around us with drifts of powdery dirt piled up in the road ditches and heaped in the lee of buildings. I remember making miniature towns in the blowdirt next to our house where it was the coolest: read, least hot!

Our little three-room house had no screens on the windows and we couldn't afford to buy them. Mother got a small roll of wire screen and tacked it outside several windows, but it helped only a little. When we opened the windows for a stray breeze, those huge yellow and green locusts, along with horse flies and wasps, would squirm in through any loose spots, looking for shade from the unrelenting heat.

Mother purchased some lacy curtains for our living room and we all enjoyed her pleasure in having something new and pretty. One hot, windy day we all went to town to take produce in to sell. Sometime while we were gone the wind blew the door open. When we arrived home, the house was swarming with grasshoppers; the floor and tabletop, the stove and beds, covered and alive. To our dismay, only a few shreds of those new curtains were hanging from the rods with grasshoppers still chewing on them. Mother sat down and cried. It took us several days to get all those locusts out of the cracks and crannies inside the house. There was just no way we could make light of that tragedy. We went for years afterward without curtains on our living room, lest they meet the same fate.

My father found some crops he could grow to provide food for the cattle he raised, so we survived. In winter 1941, when the United States went to war, machinery and fuel became expensive and hard to come by. Not that we had money to buy much. About that time, we were glad we still had some trained workhorses to help put a shoulder to the effort.

My father's parents had come to live across the road from us because my grandpa had cancer and wasn't expected to live long. Members of the extended family came often to visit, to cheer us all. They would tell stories, sing songs, dance "jig" contests, recite poems and play cards for entertainment. Some cousins from Indiana arrived in the early spring of 1942, as it started to shower. They were concerned that they might not be able to leave if it rained heavily. It had been terribly dry for so many years that we really didn't think their departure could be a problem. My father laughed and said he hoped it would rain for six weeks. And, it did. It poured for days, then it alternately showered and poured rain for weeks while we huddled around the heating stove. The card games and the dancing got less cheerful and the menus more repetitive with each day of downpour.

The amazing thing was that we began to notice that the grasshoppers had begun to die! The day of my birth, which had heralded their arrival, marked their departure eleven years later. After six weeks, the sun began to shine, the ground was drying and plants were actually growing. My father hitched a team of horses to the bumper of that Indiana car and dragged it through the muck to the closest gravel road—US Highway 16 at Vivian—about eight miles away. Although there were some grasshoppers that came to life in the following weeks, we were never again faced with those swarming waves. True to our family spirit, we celebrated that next Independence Day with songs and dancing, a rocket, and a cake with homemade ice cream.

A huge harvest of hay and grain followed that cold, rainy spring. Our neighbors gathered in that bounty with joy and we all participated in the nationwide effort at defeating foes, both in and out of our country. The banks flourished, the hoppers drowned and I was eleven.

 Grasshoppers are susceptible to a fungus, which grows under its shell at a specific temperature and humidity, causing death.

Audrey Jensen

SING ALONG WITH MITCH

Audrey Jensen

Audrey and her husband, Keith, moved to Prairie Creek in 2008. They have six sons and ten grandchildren, all miracles in their own way. She worked at the Good Sam Corporate office before retiring. Mitch Miller's TV program "Sing Along With Mitch" was a popular program the year their son, Mitch, was born. It was our theme for Christmas that year and our new baby conducted his own show.

The year was 1962. My husband and I, along with our three little boys, were happily settled on the shore of beautiful Lake Okabena in Worthington, Minnesota, eagerly looking forward to a new arrival in October. The stork had other plans and arrived two months early with a healthy four pound, nine ounce boy. We went to see him every day and his brothers loved to see him crawl out of his diapers.

We brought him home one day shy of his due date. My mother had been staying with us and went home that afternoon. Our neighbors made a visit that evening and that was when we noticed something wrong. While giving him his bottle, our conversation came to a halt. He was lying in my arms very still; it was obvious something was wrong. I started to panic trying to coax him to drink. Our neighbors went home. I got him ready for bed and he fell asleep, I watched him throughout the night to make sure he was breathing.

He never cried to be fed and his face was pale. By 5:00 a.m., I knew we had to get him back to the hospital.

Uppermost in my mind was to have him baptized. Our pastor came at 7:00 a.m. and his brothers watched in their pajamas as he was baptized.

We rushed to the local hospital and the doctor was called. Tests of all kinds were administered and the doctor referred to his condition as a "backward convulsion." The spells were more frequent throughout the day and nurses from intensive care reported that they had told the doctor on several occasions about the baby's spells. The doctor checked his vitals and could find nothing wrong.

At 4:00 p.m., the doctor advised us to get to the Mayo Clinic as soon as possible. This struck fear in me as we had never had this kind of trauma. Also, we had never been east of Worthington and we had no idea where we were going.

Our doctor instructed us to get going as soon as possible and he would make all arrangements at St. Mary's Hospital. A quick look at the map told us we would have about 260 miles to go, a five-hour drive. It was a dark and rainy night. With the cooperation of our community, we were able to get on the road about 5:30.

I held my hand under his little shirt, feeling his heartbeat and to check on his breathing. All the time in the quiet car, I kept hearing the 23rd Psalm with tears rolling down my cheeks. We were now experiencing what might be a death in our happy family.

About 30 miles down the road, I could no longer feel him breathe and I asked Keith to pull over to the side of the road. We had been advised to snap him on the bottom of his feet to stimulate his breathing. I didn't have the strength. Keith worked with him until he was over the spell only to have this happen several times as we sped toward the hospital.

By the time we got to Blue Earth, we felt we needed help. We found the emergency entrance of the hospital and a doctor answered our call. He advised us to keep going and he would advise Rochester that we were on the road. In a sympathetic voice he wished us a Merry Christmas, a rather odd greeting on October 1.

Shortly before midnight, we found the emergency entrance and my husband nearly collapsed as he rang the bell. The door opened immediately and two nurses inquired in unison, "Is this the Jensen baby?" They grabbed our son and ran with him down the hall.

We registered and went to pediatrics. We were told to get some sleep and come back in the morning, which we did.

We saw our son all hooked up with wires to his heart and his head. The doctor advised us to go back home, which we needed to do to be with our other boys. They said they would call every day and we could call them.

On the third day, the call came that our son had been near death and the cardiologist and neurologist were unable to find the cause of his behavior. Out of desperation, they administered cortisone, which brought him out of his convulsion. Cortisone is not supposed to work for 24 hours. The doctors were mystified when the shot immediately made our son well. How could this be?

On the eleventh day, we got the call to come get our baby. When we arrived, two doctors were in a very animated conversation about heart versus brain. The sweet little Filipino nurse handed our son to us and advised us to ignore the doctor's debate. She said, "It is God's miracle!" I asked what we should do if it happened again and she replied, "It won't."

And it didn't.

We returned for a final checkup at Mayo the day after Christmas. As we passed Blue Earth, we shouted, "Merry Christmas to you, Doctor, wherever you are!"

FOLLOW THE PIPER

We give a lot of credit to our neighbor, a registered nurse, who administered our baby 40 shots of cortisone. Our entire community was a blessing to us.

Our Mitch quickly caught up to his brothers. He was a star athlete, homecoming king, college graduate, a husband and father of two beautiful daughters.

 Not until about 1980, was ambulance service with EMTs available to most communities.

TO MARKET I MUST GO

Virginia Knorr

Virginia was born on a farm in Iowa. She and her husband had three children; two sons and a daughter. With a flair for fashion and retail, she went from saleslady to a buyer for a bridal shop. Sioux Falls has been her home for 70 years. Virginia moved into Prairie Creek in May of 2010.

As I was sitting in a Delta airplane headed for Dallas, Texas, I kept thinking, "How did I get here?" The flight attendants handed out the gratuitous little bottles of liquor. They were so beautiful that I kept a collection of these unopened bottles as good memories of my many flights. As the plane droned on through the night, I couldn't help but feel amazed that, I, a young widow at 45 from Rock Valley, Iowa, would be traveling around the United States as a buyer for the Bridal Department of the French Door located in Sioux Falls, South Dakota.

While I was working at Butteries Dress Shop, the owner of the French Door came to my home and asked if I'd work for him as Assistant Manager. I had two sons in college and a 13-year-old daughter at home; and after I was promised to have my summers free, we made a deal. Later, I became Manager of the Bridal Department and went to many markets and fashion shows in Dallas, Chicago, New York, and Los Angeles. We always bought high quality merchandise and I felt lucky to be able to buy anything I wanted at cost.

I sat back in the plane's seat and kept reminiscing about my first buying trip, which is one that introduced me to new and different life styles. At this one particular fashion show, we were welcomed by some of the designers. Most of them were men in white suits and each had painted fingernails, but the most shocking part was that these white suits were made of see-through polyester. It was obvious that they wore nothing underneath. I thought. "Should I look away?" or "Should I blush?" or "Should I just ignore it and get used to all kinds of fashion shows and their designers?"

I learned very quickly that the bridal gowns were chosen for price, quality, and workmanship. We would try to carry the inexpensive Mori Lee line, the middle Alfred Angelo line, and the more expensive Priscilla and Bianchi lines. For the head pieces, the Mori Lee was low end, T&G was the middle, and Priscilla and Bianchi were more spendy, but very beautiful. As I sat there in the plane, all those gorgeous gowns came to mind.

The better houses had showrooms and all gowns were modeled by girls with flawless figures, so when buying I had to be very careful and remember that I was buying the gown, not the model, as these girls could make any gown look beautiful. Some of the gowns were too revealing for the Midwest, but we also had to remember the fashion-conscious girls, who would prefer a more daring gown. All those gorgeous gowns came to mind.

Because styles would vary from house to house, we would start at the low end for our samples and work up to the better houses. This way, we could enjoy all gowns shown. All day, we would write descriptions and at night after dinner, our work would begin while our memory would carry us back to the show room; and we could still picture that particular gown. After a week at market, we would look back at our descriptions and see if we could find "Knock offs." These were dresses that were too expensive, so later we might find that certain style at a different house and at a lower price. This often happened, as designers are known for copying designs.

When future brides would come in, we would always show middle of the line for price first. From that point, we could tell what a girl was looking for in a bridal gown. Maybe she would want more detail of embroidery and lace, a more revealing dress or one with sleeves. We could soon determine what price she would want to pay and then we knew if we should go to the better line or to the less expensive line. I can just picture one particular gown. It was very unusual as it looked like it came from or was designed in the '20s. We passed it up the first few days at market, but I couldn't get it out of my mind so the last day of market, I asked my employer if he would consider it. He agreed and we sold 29 of these gowns, which is a lot for one style. Here was an example of girls seeing something they hadn't had in mind, but the price was right and the design was unusual.

On one buying trip to New York, my associate and I went out to eat dinner and when we came back, we noticed our hotel room had been disturbed. My good pair of beige shoes was missing and my associate was also missing her pair of beige shoes. We called the police and were told that it obviously was an inside job and that it had happened quite often. These hotels were located in the garment district where the fashion markets were located. It seemed that during these thieving sprees only certain items of a certain color were taken.

While enjoying my plane ride, I kept thinking how much fun I had in managing the Bridal Department especially when I was allowed to expand it by including fancy undergarments and other pretty things. I was told if these were successful, I would get a bonus. I did get that bonus.

I put my head back and tried to relax as I fumbled with my diamond ring. All of a sudden, I remembered one wealthy woman who came into the store and was going through the clothes that were displayed on the rack. "Oh, no," she exclaimed, "my diamond is gone." She was still wearing the ring, but the diamond itself was gone. She was sure it was still in the setting while she was in the car, so I quickly went outside to see if it might be beside the car. It was a snowy day with snow all over the parking lot, so I was afraid we could never find it even if she did lose it in the parking lot. As I went toward the car, I saw something sparkling in the sun on the top of the snow. I quickly picked it up and it was her three-carat diamond. She was one happy person!

Of course, I couldn't help think about some of the sad and disappointing situations. One day a pretty little girl came into the store. She had ordered her bridal dress and all the clothes for her wedding party. She was in tears and her mother was trying to console her as she told me her daughter's fiancé had called off the wedding because he was afraid to get married. So here we were with all those wedding gowns that were not refundable and could do nothing about it.

Another rather chubby girl was five months pregnant and wanted to order her wedding gown. The date was set for two months later when she would be seven months pregnant. I tried to figure out what size she might need on her wedding day. Then I ordered the dress with stipulations that it could be altered or enlarged. We found a company that would make the dress with expandable seams. What a relief that all went well.

Then I thought of the little girl from Rock Valley, Iowa, who ordered her gowns in time so they would arrive a few days before the wedding. Sometimes the bridal companies were not on time and this time everything came on time except the bride's hat. The day before the wedding she came to the store and no hat. What was I to do? Then I offered her the sample hat to wear. That evening, after she left, her hat arrived; so I drove to Rock Valley that night and delivered the precious cargo so the bride could wear her own bridal hat the next day—her wedding day. To see the bride-to-be so excited and thankful for this little act is what made my job rewarding.

As the plane slowed down and prepared to land, I collected my things and wondered what experiences I would have during the next two weeks. The anticipation and excitement of going to market never gets old!

 Department store buyers today have college degrees and internships. Virginia's energy and natural talent served her well.

RAINDROPS

Lynn Assimacopoulos

What things those tiny mirrors of life do see,
On the world of emotions they fall.
The scintillate spectrum of their surfaces
Absorb impressions manifold.
The hate and fear that denies and blinds
Breeds disfavor and bitterness.

Hate between people anonymous to each other.
Fear embalmed in suspicion
And mingled with misgiving.
Love inflamed in passion,
Love out of pure love.

A heart that cannot love
Can neither serve, nor act, nor function.
Joy expressed in laughter or in tears.
Delight in others and self delight.
Hidden joy, insincere job.
Joy for mere sake of life itself.

Sorrow from without and within,
That which kills and strengthens.
Death nourishes sorrow.
Repentance ebbs it.
Unimportant sorrow,
Better left for bigger things.
Sorrow expressed only in silence.
Reflection on these tiny mirrors
Can enhance the vision of the conscious world.
Like the truly great—
They absorb, fall and best of all—
Learn to rise again.

Bon's reception room in Indonesia

EMBASSY TALES

Bon Slade

Bon was born in Eastern Iowa on the shore of the mighty Mississippi. Her teachers saw her as a dreamer. The dreams remained as she traveled the world and met fascinating people, lived in Third World countries and met the challenges of unexpected life experiences perhaps greater than the dreams she had as a child. Bon moved to Prairie Creek in 2009.

I had my first airplane ride in my twenties. I was on my way to Madrid, Spain, to train Spanish personnel to take over jobs held by American civilians at Torrejon Air Force Base. We'd left Headquarters, Strategic Air Command (SAC), Omaha. But upon our approach landing in Bermuda, we mini-crashed. The pilots worked frantically to regain power. We circled a few times and finally came in for a safe landing after missing by inches going into the dreaded Bermuda Triangle.

I was still shaking when the time came for me to fly back to SAC six months later. I sure wasn't relishing flying again, but as it turned out, our trip home was a delightful flight. We stopped in Paris—it was April.

A nice Air Force captain sitting next to me just happened to have a sporty Ford Thunderbird parked at Orley Field in Paris. He took me on a glorious tour of the city. We stopped at an outdoor café on the Champs Elysees

FOLLOW THE PIPER

where I drank a "Ricard." It tasted like licorice, but I found out later it is an aphrodisiac banned in the U.S.

I did make my flight, however.

Several months after my return to SAC, I met a newly arrived colonel and married him a year later. He was eventually assigned as the Air/Defense Attaché at the American Embassy, Djakarta, Indonesia, on the island of Java.

In preparation for his assignment, we both attended language school in Washington, D.C. for over a year. We also studied the customs of the 5,000 island archipelago. We had to take table service (glassware, dishes, silverware) for 400 guests as diplomats entertain and are entertained nearly every night. During this time, our two sons were one and two years old.

The help of nine servants in Indonesia eased my transition from a 'lil old girl from Iowa to a responsible helpmate to my husband by gathering pertinent information from coffees, teas, and luncheons.

An embassy isn't all dull and serious. Each year we were brought back to the states for classes in detecting terrorists, bombings, threats, and suspects to the embassy.

One humorous event occurred when American Ambassador Green to Indonesia was entertaining President Kennedy's Cabinet as guests. We attaché wives were always required to be helpers at diplomatic functions.

Mrs. Green was needlepointing while waiting for luncheon guests. I was chosen as her handmaiden. Suddenly, she exclaimed, "Bon, I have sewn my needlepoint to my skirt; the guests are arriving for lunch, what will I do?"

I told her not to worry, I would walk in front of her, seat her; then get a pair of scissors to cut off the sewing. It worked. Governor Averell Harriman, Attorney General Bobby Kennedy and Defense Secretary Robert McNamara, along with the other guests, didn't notice a thing.

Another time in Indonesia, my husband's bachelor deputy asked me to order his Christmas cards—not an easy task in a Muslim country. I found a small printing shop, wrote out the instructions for the name to be printed in red on the card. Sure enough, the captain's name, along with "printed in red" was on the card. He sent them out that way.

At one of my luncheons I asked the houseboy, Marcidi, to please serve the wine to my guests—he did—but it was colored water from my collection of fancy bottles. He thought it was wine.

On a trip to the gorgeous, only Hindu island in Indonesia, "Bali," my husband was flying the embassy plane with Mrs. Green and attaché wives. Mrs. Green was very proud of the fact she was a "Winthrop" from Massachusetts and that her clothes were designed by famous New York and French designers. She was standing in the middle of the plane holding out her dress label and asked, "Bon, who designed this?"

I couldn't resist. "Sears and Roebuck," I answered.

She must have forgiven me (or gotten even with me) because next she appointed me chairperson of the Embassy's Fourth of July celebration with 4,000 invitations. She wanted hot dog and hamburger stands built on the Embassy grounds with red, white and blue lights strung throughout the trees. All this, and the food had to be flown in from Singapore.

The Ambassador of Singapore just happened to be Frank Gailbraith from Sisseton, South Dakota. Needless to say, we received very good service.

At this time, our three-year-old son, Billy, was evacuated from Indonesia to the American Air Force base hospital in the Philippines. He had acute amoebic dysentery. His father flew him there leaving me with my chairperson duties and son Mark, who was covered with infected mosquito bites. Both sons recovered, but I am not sure Mrs. Green ever did.

You see, when all those lights were turned on at the Embassy grounds, it caused an electrical blackout. We had a dark Fourth of July for a while until the generator kicked in. Remember, we were in a Third World country.

We lived in Indonesia during a coup d'etat. President Sukarno was out of favor. The Communists wanted control.

The American wives and children were evacuated back to the states. I left my home, belongings and husband, not knowing if I would see him again.

When the situation calmed down, we were sent back. Bad timing! The coup started again. We had bullets dropping on our patio couch. In the house behind us, generals were shot, rolled up in a rug and carted away. Streams ran with real blood. Our children were escorted to an International pre-school under armed guard.

After six years, our supposedly two-year tour ended. A day never went by that I wasn't homesick for my country.

My husband retired after 30 years of military service. We returned to his hometown of Canton, South Dakota, and raised the boys. Billy went off and graduated from West Point. Mark attended South Dakota State and joined the Navy for 20 years as a deep-sea diver.

At the age of 50, I decided to go back to school to regain my administrative skills. I took an eight-hour Foreign Service test, passed and was assigned to the American Embassy in Beijing, China, as Assistant to the Public Affairs Officer (PAO). My husband came along as my dependent. We were diplomats together again. This was shortly after the Cultural Revolution ended and China was opening up to the world.

After two years, I was assigned to the Embassy PAO in Pretoria, South Africa, near Johannesburg. Thankfully, apartheid ended shortly after. My last posting was with the PAO at The Hague, near Amsterdam, in the Netherlands.

I retired from Foreign Service after 11 years, plus 9 years civil service. I have often been asked where I liked living the best. My answer—Sioux Falls, South Dakota.

 Dream big and accept challenges.

Connie's home at 29 Railway Street in Canada

CONCETTA

Connie McLauchlan

Connie was born in Canada in 1925. Her husband was transferred to Sioux Falls. They and two of their children made the move, while the two oldest stayed in Canada. Connie became a U.S. citizen in 1983, and worked in retail. She moved to Prairie Creek in 2006.

My parents both came from the same small village in Sicily, yet they never met until they immigrated to Hamilton, Ontario, Canada. I was the youngest of five children. My father worked for the railroad and my mother's responsibility was to "keep the house and rear the children." The railroad taught my father English. My mother would allow only English spoken in the house and that is how she learned English.

Our house was on Railway Street, where many bootleggers, racketeers, and Mafia lived. I remember it, through the eyes of a child, as being exciting, but looking back, I understand why my mother secretly saved money to get us into a better neighborhood. Her fear was not for our safety, but, as a parent, she wanted a better life for us. She also worried my brothers would fall prey to less than a reputable lifestyle.

My days were spent wandering down Railway Street where there was always adventure. Sometimes a bootlegger would pay me a dime or two to look out for detectives, who warned the bootleggers when a raid was coming. During the day, the detectives would go through the motions of checking on the bootleggers, but, at night, we could see them drinking with the bootleggers, including Mr. Roughhead, the head detective.

In our neighborhood, Johnny was one of the more intimidating men. He used his car repair shop as a front for more Mafia business. Years later, Johnny was shot while the ladies were sitting on their verandas. The Mafia ladies had little bells on their laps and they would ring them as a warning to those in the house.

Johnny's mother was a bootlegger with a long skirt and heavy apron to keep her bootleg money concealed. They often kept liquor in our back shed. I spent afternoons on her veranda, visiting, and when I was confirmed in the Catholic Church, my mother asked her to stand up for me. I remember with delight the beautiful doll she gave me as a gift. Money was tight, which made the doll even more precious.

The day came when we moved off Railway Street. Now we were exposed to unfamiliar cultures: Scottish, English and Irish families. I stood out like a sore thumb because my name was Concetta. I was dressed in red bloomers and wore hoop earrings. The other families looked down on us because we were Italian and they called us Wops.

When I was about ten, I went with my mother to market The wagon was full of vegetables, fruit, and a live chicken. The chicken jumped out of the wagon and I had to chase after it and catch it. Many families were watching and I was totally embarrassed. After that, the kids called me "Chicken Girl" for a long time. I begged to be called Connie so I could fit in.

One day, my mother received a very chilling Sicilian Black Hand symbol, which was a Mafia sign. Without telling Dad, she went back to the old neighborhood and gave the letter to Johnny. He told her to forget it and he would take care of it. It was explained to Mom that while Dad was working on the railroad, the Mafia asked him to do something for them that he refused to do. We never heard from them again.

We also learned that Rocco Parry, a prominent Mafioso, who often walked down Railway Street in his finery, was found on the bottom of the Hamilton Bay, with a block of cement.

Railway Street is no longer peppered with the Mafia. It is now a friendly, inviting neighborhood. But, in my mind, it's not much different from what I remember.

I can see my cousins who lived across the street and relatives coming to visit us. We slept behind the stove when it was cold. I can see my father coming home from the railroad with frost in his mustache and my mother chopping wood for the cook stove. I can imagine my two sisters sleeping in one bed with me and my two brothers in the other bed; and when the weather turned cold, we all slept together.

Even though we were raised on Railway Street, our parents made sure we knew right from wrong. We don't think of the racketeers as being bad people even though they did bad things. They were friends to us at the time.

 In life, sometimes it's important to have friends in low places.

Alice and her mother, Leona Granberg

THE BRIDE'S FIRST DONUTS

Alice Mikkelson

Alice taught country school for one year and moved to Sioux Falls, where she met her husband. They bought a trailer house and lived on the road with a construction company. Moving back to Sioux Falls, her husband managed a new Texaco and Alice was the bookkeeper. They had seven children. Alice moved into Prairie Creek in 2006.

Both my mother and my mother-in-law were excellent cooks and neither had a job outside the home. They cooked, cleaned and did all the traditional things a wife was expected to do. My experience with most of these tasks was the two years of high school home economics classes.

The classes touched on cooking, sewing and home management. We learned how to make stuffed pork chops and I sewed a dress for a three-year-old cousin. Because this was before food coupons, we learned how to get the best food bargains.

Mother must have thought that I was learning what I should know so we skipped that part of motherly advice. Her way was a pinch of that and stir it until it sticks to something. Mom's cooking was always successful.

Mom's donuts were considered the best! She made them every morning at the café she and my dad owned. I asked her to write down the recipe for me, which she did.

We had received a fryer for a wedding gift and donuts would be the first goody cooked in it. I mixed the dough, worked in the flour, rolled them out on a thin layer of flour and let them rise.

Carefully, I slid the first donut into the hot grease and waited for it to come to the top, but it didn't. I fished it out and turned the cooker up a bit thinking that would help. It didn't. They turned dark as they laid on the bottom of the cooker.

I tried some holes with the same result. My husband was sitting on the couch watching. He took a bite and promptly spit it out and said, "These are like rocks! Give them to the dogs." I threw them out into the yard where the dogs were. They turned around and walked away, they wouldn't even touch them.

That was the last straw. I called my mother, half crying, to tell her what had happened. "Now, now dear, let's check the recipe, you must have read it wrong," she suggested. I read her the recipe and she wanted to know how much baking powder I put in.

"None," I replied.

I heard my mother sigh as she said, "It's the baking powder that makes them rise."

 Home economics classes have been replaced by classes that include a wide spectrum of life skills, which appeal to both boys and girls.

THE GYPSY WOMAN

Theresa Collins

Theresa moved into Prairie Creek in 2007. She and her husband were chiropractors in Turner County, South Dakota, for many years. They raised a family of five girls and two boys. Her mother-in-law is 110 and her mother lived to be 104.

My father saw them coming and came into the house to make sure the entire family was there. We went to the front porch and watched the Gypsy caravan approach the house. They had been there in previous years so we knew what to expect. They were beggars, but people still remembered stories of children missing. Whether or not it was true, the Gypsy people were often the suspects. Parents made sure the children knew their reputation and cautioned them to be aware of all strangers.

As they approached, my father was on his way to meet them. "Please, Father, may I go with you?" I asked. "I would so like to see the pretty woman you talk with." Father held my arm tightly and asked me to stay close by.

The pretty woman came out of the covered wagon, which was pulled by a team of horses. Later, we counted seven wagons in the caravan.

The woman who approached my father was of dark skin and dressed in colorful clothing. Beautiful jewelry covered her arms, ears and neck; the belt around her dress was silver.

She said, "We are hungry and our animals need food. Do you have some food for us and our animals? We don't need much, but could we have one chicken?" She spoke in English, but the use of another language made her words sound sophisticated. I was charmed by her and I didn't understand how they could be dangerous. She was charming, mysterious, and beautiful.

My Father spoke to me. "Theresa, get this woman one chicken and bring it to me."

When I returned with the chicken, the woman spoke again. "We are a big family; could we please have one more chicken?" Again, Father asked me to bring him another chicken.

While I was away, I learned the woman had asked for some oats for the horses and the cow. As I returned with the second chicken, I saw them gathering some oats in a sack and a few ears of corn.

The Gypsy woman thanked my Father and handed him his gold pocket watch, which he didn't even know she had stolen. He always carried the watch in his bib overalls.

They came into our farm to turn around and we watched them as they made their way down the driveway. Two people sat on the front bench, but we could see other people under the canvas that arched over the wagon. Mother looked at us children and firmly said, "See the children, we tell you that they steal children." Chickens were prisoners in the crates tied to the wagons; and cows, young calves and several colts were tethered to the back of the wagons.

The next morning, our uncle came over to tell us that they, too, had been visited by the Gypsy beggars. He allowed them to stay the night in his pasture. Shortly after sunset, he walked to the edge of his grove to listen to their music and watch them sing, dance and swirl about. They had gathered some firewood to start a beautiful fire.

Some time later, we heard a neighbor boy was missing; a boy of about fourteen. A search was conducted, but the boy could not be found. There were no clues as to why he would run away. His family was distraught beyond words and alerted the county sheriff.

Finally, came the good news. The Gypsies had kidnapped him and camped the second night about 25 miles away. The theory was that they had traveled all night and the next day. During the second night, the boy was able to break away. He ran as fast as he could through the tall corn and hid out there so he wouldn't be found.

He used the moon at night to keep him on a steady path. He traveled through cornfields and avoided situations where he might be seen. He finally found some landmarks that he recognized and found his way home.

The word spread rapidly, but the young man remained cautious the rest of his life. He disliked going to town and other places where there were crowds of people. His Gypsy experience stayed with him for his entire life.

As for me, I knew the Gypsy life was not for me.

Ms. Nightingale of the Plains at her
"Beulah Langenfeld Day" Reception

MS. NIGHTINGALE OF THE PLAINS

Beulah Langenfeld

Beulah was married to Joe, a salesman. They had seven children, four girls and three boys. Five are in the medical field, one is a Nuclear Technologist, and one works in insurance. Beulah's husband passed away in 2007, and she moved to Prairie Creek in 2009.

Being one of ten children raised on a farm near Henry, South Dakota, I learned to work hard at an early age. We had chores that had to be done before playtime. I used to love riding out to the fields with my brother on a flatbed or a hayrack to pick up hay for the animals. One particular day, I was wearing a brand new pair of shoes and ran to get a ride on the hayrack. When my brother said "Whoa" to the horses, I jumped off the wagon, and the wagon wheel went over my foot and broke the strap on my new shoes. I don't remember getting any sympathy! The broken snap on the new shoe got the sympathy.

In order to go to high school in Henry, I worked for Dr. Lockwood and his wife, who was an invalid. I was paid to live in their home and take care of Mrs. Lockwood. This stirred in me a desire to work in the medical field. In high school, I worked as an aide in the Lutheran Hospital in Watertown, South Dakota. Later, I attended the Bartron School of Nursing in Watertown. As part of this training, I was given the opportunity to work in pediatrics and orthopedics in Rochester, Minnesota. At that time,

Rochester was a very small city, in fact, there was very little there. There was only one place to go out to eat and that was out in the country.

I started working as a nurse at the Watertown Clinic. In fact, I was always a clinic nurse. In 1947, Dr. Bartron went to Clark, South Dakota, to open a clinic and he invited me to go with him as his nurse. I ran the clinic alone except for two afternoons a week when a physician came over from Watertown. I administered shots and general nursing, took care of accidents, did physical checkups, and provided aid to almost anyone who came into the clinic except those who were sent to the hospital. I was later given the title of Physician's Assistant and was on call 24 hours a day, seven days a week. I experienced many different cases and all of them were so important to me, as my passion was to help those who were hurting. In 1990, I was given the South Dakota Academy of Physician's Assistants award in recognition of service.

Working alone in the clinic was stressful at first, but it soon became routine. One night a married couple came in amidst an awful blizzard. The doctor was not in and I had to deliver the baby alone. The clinic was equipped with all the necessary equipment, which helped me feel more at ease with the many babies I delivered over the years. Another incident occurred while one couple from Colorado was visiting in Clark, South Dakota. Their little boy was bitten on the face by a dog and they brought him to the clinic where I was working alone. I wanted them to take the child to the hospital, but the grandparents, who were my patients, insisted that I do the stitching and kept saying, "You can do it. You can do it." Very reluctantly, I did. I gave the little guy a local anesthetic and very carefully stitched his face. The little boy, who was about six or seven years old, did not cry once. His face turned out exceptionally well and the stitching left very little scar. They were so happy with the results.

FOLLOW THE PIPER

One unusual assignment happened when a terrible tornado came through Clark. Among all the destruction, one lady died and I was called to the funeral home because the mortician asked me to suture the lady's face so he could apply makeup on the body. Following the storm that night, I had to give tetanus shots to everyone by flashlight since there was no electricity due to the storm.

I was chosen by the county commissioners to become the County Coroner. Some of the cases were sad and some were gruesome. One elderly lady fell and broke her hip, and as the doctor and I were getting her ready to go to the hospital, she died in the clinic. One young boy committed suicide. He was living with his relatives and one day he laid on the couch and shot himself in the head. We found brains hanging on the ceiling. The scene is unexplainable. A man in the southern part of the county was in a storeroom near a mattress spring. We found him with his brains hanging from the mattress spring. A married lady tried a self-abortion with a coat hanger and died. This was a very traumatic time as it took a number of weeks before she died and the odor was almost unbearable. These experiences, and many more like them, were the most difficult and saddest of my nursing career.

One funny experience happened one night when my assistant and I, as the County Coroner, were called to the southern part of the county. There had been a terrible car accident and one person was taken to the hospital and the other was pronounced dead and left in the car. When we came to the scene, we could not find the fatality. We looked in the cornfield, in the car, and all over. We could not leave the scene without a body, so we spent the entire night looking for him and in the morning we saw this "fatality" walking toward us. He was dead all right, "DEAD DRUNK." The rescue crew thought he was dead, but later he had crawled away and slept off his drunkenness. This happened on Holy Saturday, so we said, "No need for us to go to Mass now, it is too late." I answered, "Why should we, we already saw a resurrection."

In 1976, the Clark Medical Center and Dr. Bartron honored me with "Beulah Day" for 43 years of service. I just about missed this event when my daughter's Arabian horse cut its leg on some glass. When she called, we raced out to the farm where she and the horse were located. We got the horse to the vet and just made it back into town for my own party. I officially retired from the medical field in 1995.

 A dedicated nurse is a gift to mankind.

Beulah Langenfeld Day

By Diane Warkenthien

There's a woman in our hearts today
Who, like a blossoming flower,
Has grown to care for all of us
Through each striving hour.

Unfolding each her buds, she would,
To comfort each and all
Pulling thorns from needy ones
With problems great and small.

With tributes to the needy ones
We now begin to see—
That her unselfishness to all of us
Was of great necessity.

Lies in her roots a secret
As ancient as the hills.
Her steady hands, her knowing work,
Her intentional good will.

With fragile scent at her throat
Her words are comforting and bright.
Though rising early, working hard,
And retiring late at night.

So what's to be the reason
That we're gathered here today?
To shower her with gifts of love—
It's Beulah Langenfeld Day!

It's her day.

Teenage Lifeguards at the Britton Pool

A HOLE FOR THE FUTURE

Marilyn Peters

Marilyn grew up in Britton, SD, a small town on the Continental Divide between Hudson Bay and the Gulf of Mexico. She and her husband, Emerald, farmed for 50 years northeast of town. They had cropland on the "flats" and pasture and hay land in the hills for cattle. Their children, Scott and Teresa, live in Sioux Falls, as does Marilyn since moving to Prairie Creek in 2009. She has five granddaughters and one great-granddaughter.

Long before the stock market crash in 1929, South Dakota was feeling the effects of a depression post-war economy with fallen farm prices and land values. By 1930, there were already nearly 23,000 farm foreclosures; the crisis became overwhelming during the "Dust Bowl" years when it became clear that any relief would need to come through federal government assistance.

My first childhood memory is such a vivid one that I have wondered a bit about why I recall it in such detail. My mother and I were walking past the Carnegie Library at the north end of Main Street and we watched a large number of men digging a very big hole. I was not yet four years old in June of 1933, but I remember the feeling of excitement I felt when I was told it was going to be a swimming pool.

Of course, I was too young to understand that the men digging the pool were working under the first federal program designed to alleviate poverty during the Great

Depression—the Federal Emergency Relief Administration (FERA) passed by Congress only weeks before on May 12th. It was the first of numerous special programs such as CWP, PWA, and WPA to boost the economy. Our small town was very proactive in studying ways to utilize the funding sources through grants and loans.

It was Britton's Commercial Club that spearheaded many projects. As its secretary and city auditor, my daddy was one of three sent to Lake Preston to confer with officials there about their "very fine pool." A prompt decision was made by the city council to build an oval shaped pool, 120' by 60'; and by June 21st, 50 men were put to work in two shifts at 20 cents an hour digging, just as I remember. The newspaper reported that it was being done in this manner to "give employment to as many men as possible. While it may not be completed in as short a time as if machinery was used, work is nevertheless progressing at a rapid rate and a few weeks will see it completed." By July 20th they started pouring cement and work was started on the bathhouse, which had seven windows on the poolside and one on each end (not the typical austere plan of others built during this period).

The following year, Britton celebrated its Fifty Year Jubilee. Opening day for the pool was June 9, 1934. I also have a clear memory of that day. Mom went inside the fenced in area around the "little side" and stood by the edge as I fearlessly climbed into the shallow water, only to loose my footing and start spinning around under water! My mother's cry for help brought a lifeguard, who righted me, and I was soon walking around the edge of this wonderful pool that became my home away from home for many years.

The pool provided me with many hours to hang out with my friends. We rested between swimming and games on towels (no outsized ones in those days) on the warm cement and on the bench over the library basement steps. I became qualified as both a junior and senior lifesaver and later earned my water safety instructor's certification (WSI). The highlight of my teen years was during WWII when help was at a premium, so my best friend and I were the only lifeguards and taught swimming for the month of August in 1944. After high school, I was in charge of a Red Cross program that included 400 swimmers from all of Marshall County. At NSTC in Aberdeen, I taught a men's beginner class and the next summer had an adult beginner's class in Britton. Later, as a high school PE teacher, I also worked with high school girls who had never had the opportunity to swim.

And it all began with Britton's community providing for its struggling poor, and having the foresight to invest in the future.

 A childhood memory of a caring community blossoms throughout the years.

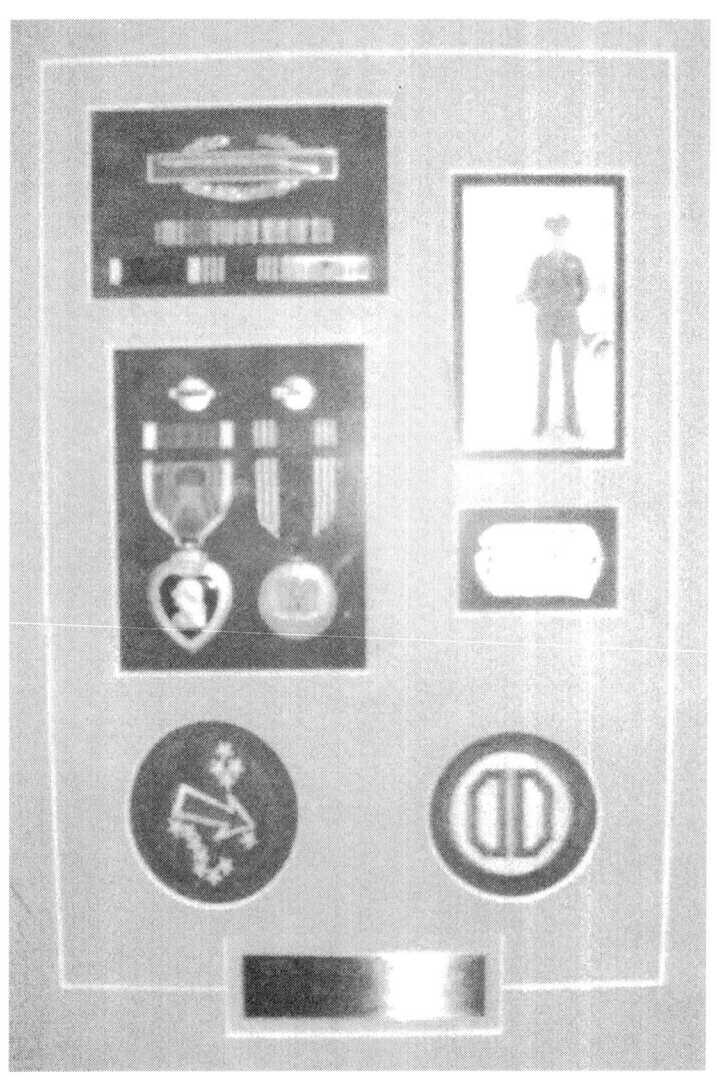

Stan's Medals, including the Purple Heart

ANSWERING MY COUNTRY'S CALL

Stan Lovro

Stan graduated from Sioux Falls Washington High School and entered the Army on November 17, 1942. His marriage of 57 years brought two sons and two daughters into the family. Stan worked three years as a banker and assumed a position with Insurance Services Office, a fire and casualty company, for 33 years. He moved into Prairie Creek in July 2008.

Upon induction into the Army on November 17, 1942, Stan received basic training and advanced training as a gunner in the 31st Infantry Division in various states in the USA; and shipped out on a Dutch Freighter converted to a troop ship from Newport News, Virginia, on March 1, 1944. Sailing through the Panama Canal, the ship zigzagged for 30 days across the Pacific before arriving at Oro Bay in New Guinea. His troops were reviewed by General McArthur at one point in time.

There was more training and we later advanced to position near an airstrip, encountering Japanese. On August 6, 1944, Stan, manning a 50-caliber machine gun with his buddy, was struck by a fragment from a Japanese mortar shell. The fragment entered near his right shoulder and exited his chest; and a fragment also hit near his right wrist. His buddy was killed. They were found somewhat later by medics and Stan was treated at a tent hospital. More time was spent in New Guinea before being shipped back to the USA on November 21, 1944, for further treatment at Letterman General Hospital, San Francisco; Bushnell General Hospital, Brigham City, Utah; and Percy Jones Hospital, Fort Custer, Michigan.

After discharge from Fort Custer, Stan was assigned active duty and worked at registering veterans returning from Europe until the war was over. He was honorably discharged December 14, 1945. Corporal Stan Lovro was awarded the Purple Heart.

Fast forward to 2010: At coffee in the Prairie Creek Library; the discussion was about the patriotism we felt during the Second World War. The following subjects reflect the unity and determination of all of us as people, communities, and nation. Sacrifice was the key word.

*Country school children were asked to pick milkweed pods containing fluffy seeds that could be used to pack life jackets for the Navy.

*Community gatherings were regularly held to sell War Bonds to finance the war. Often, talent shows were held to attract a crowd.

*Government ration stamps were issued limiting purchase of commodities like gas, tires, food and clothing. We cooperated so our boys and girls could get home as soon as possible in victory.

*Hollywood sent their stars to entertain the troops at home and abroad.

*Sioux Falls had a radio school for military training. We, like other towns and cities across the nation, held dances with homemade treats and invited the boys into our homes to show our appreciation.

*School age children were sent to school with a dime to purchase a stamp that could be pasted into a stamp book. When it reached $18.75, it was invested as a war bond and would later be worth $25.

*Victory gardens were everywhere and mothers were taught how to preserve the bounty from the gardens.

*Mothers hung banners from their windows, one for each soldier serving at home or abroad. Special banners with a gold star were hung for those who lost their lives.

*School age children were taught the hymns of all the service units and sung them with pride. Small plays were given to tell the story of brave soldiers who were fighting for us.

*Church services included prayers for victory and a safe return of our soldiers.

*Road trips and purchases of commodities were put off if possible to help the war effort.

*Nearly everyone drove 35 miles an hour to save on gas and tires.

*Farmers donated the use of their pickups to haul scrap iron into collection points.

 Medals are earned with honor in the fight for freedom.

Ardeth Rang's Capping Ceremony

LIVING THE AMERICAN DREAM

Ardeth Rang

As a little girl, Ardeth nursed her sick dolls and teddy bear, but her dream came true when she graduated from nurse's training. She and her husband, Norm, have three sons and one daughter. They moved into Prairie Creek in 2008.

"**A**rdit Ellopha, vachca vant for Kipits?" (Christmas) asked my father in his broken German/English, when I was seven years old. I was quick to answer, "A nurse's kit!" for I always played nurse.

My mother fashioned a large white handkerchief into an apron and headband using red tape for the crosses. A cardboard box held cinnamon candy for pills, a stethoscope, bandages from an old sheet and fudgesicle sticks for tongue depressors.

I grew up near Wall Lake and attended country school. My father was a 4H leader and under his direction his three children raised livestock and exhibited at the fair. It was there that I met my future husband, who thought I was "kinda silly and much too young."

My family and I loved living on the farm and as we children grew, so did our responsibilities. Chores on the farm consisted of the following activities:

*Feeding animals and keeping barns and chicken coops clean

FOLLOW THE PIPER

*Chopping weeds and cockleburs out of the corn fields
*Removing rocks from the fields, a very hard job
*Weeding the garden and canning the fruits and vegetables
*Fixing fences and horse harnesses, a rainy day job
*Learning to sew, cook, and bake
*Cleaning the house was an endless job
*Helping neighbors when they needed it
*Hanging the washed clothes outside on the line, winters included
*Ironing with old-fashioned "sad" irons.

I took piano lessons and sang with my sister and one of my brothers within the community, an activity I also enjoyed as an adult. Roller-skating at Wall Lake was THE place to have fun.

On August 10, 1948, I was packed early and ready to join my church and school friend where we enrolled in nurse's training. It was hard work and I loved it. Money was tight, but I didn't need much to stay happy. I was living my dream.

Initially, student nurses on probation wore big black bows on their striped uniforms. "Probie ties" kept the doctors from asking us questions about our patients, which we wouldn't know.

Certain classes required high scores plus the ability to demonstrate the skill to the instructor before we could receive our "CAP." Capping ceremonies were very special. My roommate and I sang in the chorus and a doctor delivered an inspirational address. We carried Florence Nightingale lamps with a lit candle as our caps were placed on our heads. It was my 19th birthday. My dream: one step closer.

One by one, more difficult "nursing arts" and procedures were taught. One of the most memorable rotations was working for three months in a mental hospital. There were only a few meds available and shock therapy was the major treatment.

While I was in nurse's training, my future husband was fighting World War II. When he returned, he was able to attend college under the GI bill. Chemistry, not the kind one studies at college, was at work between us, but marriage had to be delayed for three years until I graduated from nurse's training.

I was a nurse for 45 years, the last 15 at Good Samaritan Center where I served as Director of Nursing and Staff Development Coordinator. Norm's livelihood was automotive sales and service and he taught "tune up" at Lincoln High School.

Dedication to serving others and making a career choice that brought challenges and successes led to the fulfillment of the American Dream. I believe graduation from nurse's training was the key to my career and the lock was a good marriage. And, now I ask, "Who would ever believe we would be fortunate enough to live at Prairie Creek?"

In the late '50s, nurses began wearing scrubs and capping ceremonies became a thing of the past.

?????

Lynn Assimacopoulos

It is so hard
I do not know
In which direction
I should go
For life has dealt me
One big blow—AMBIVALENCE!!

ORDER FORM

Mail Order Form To:		Keith Jensen
				4400 W Creekside Dr.
				Sioux Falls, SD 57106

Follow the Piper
Through True Life Stories of a Century
					$14.00 ea
ISBN: 978-0-9833526-1-7			.84 sales tax ea

S&H per quantity: $3.00 for 1 – 3 books

Enclosed is check or money order for: $_____

Payable to "Follow the Piper"

NAME: _____

ADDRESS:_____

_____

Made in the USA
Charleston, SC
16 May 2011